AND

SEW

IT

BEGINS

The Intricate Pattern
of
Incest

By Debbie Roxborough

****

Book One in the series

SHADOWS OF THE MIND

ISBN 0-7414-5721-0

Editor - Talene Harvee

Cover Designer - Andrew Roxborough

Published by:

INFINITY
PUBLISHING.COM

1094 New DeHaven Street, Suite 100
West Conshohocken, PA 19428-2713
Info@buybooksontheweb.com
www.buybooksontheweb.com
Toll-free (877) BUY BOOK
Local Phone (610) 941-9999
Fax (610) 941-9959

Printed in the United States of America

Published January 2010

Dedicated to...

my mother, who suffered the same kind of abuse, but because of the times of her generation was deprived of the knowledge I was graciously granted to stand up for myself and who filled me with her love and great spirit. For my grandmother who shared with me her love of crafts and through which I found my salvation, my sanity and my road back to God. And last but not least, for my children, my grandchildren, their future children and all children of earth who might find themselves in similar circumstances. May they find their own strength, courage and wisdom in my story.

ACKNOWLEDGMENTS

I would like to thank everyone who helped make this book possible.

First and foremost, one of my best friends and Editor Talene Harvee, without whom it would not have worked out the way I wanted it to.

My children for their patience and understanding while I spent countless hours working on it.

Phoenix Community Works Foundation for taking my project under their wing in order to raise the funds necessary to complete and publish my manuscript.

A special thanks to my dear friends Bridget LaForest and Tiziana Greco for their help with the proof reading and editing. And of course, I thank God and my angels for helping me through it all and guiding me back to the light.

FOREWORD

Hitting Rock Bottom

Several years ago, at the suggestion of my youngest daughter, and as I neared my 50th birthday, I decided to write a book about my life. What was particularly interesting about my life was that there always seemed to be some kind of drama going on and I knew some very interesting people. By my thirties I had pretty much hit rock bottom - or so I thought. As it turned out there was still a long way to go!

On the outside everything appeared "normal". I seemed happy and confident. My life looked like it was great. My children and I lived in a beautiful house with a man who loved us dearly and gave us whatever we wanted or needed. He had a good job and I ran a home-based business that allowed me to be home with my kids. What more could I ask for? My closest friends however, knew that something was amiss. Even they had no idea just how bad things were on the inside.

The truth was, I felt totally lost and alone, with a rage burning deep inside me. I wasn't sure what the rage was about, or where it had come from, but I was constantly aware of its presence. Most of the time I was able to keep up the happy front, but at the first sign of anyone trying to change or control me, I could feel the rage bubbling to the surface. It even happened when I saw anyone trying to control another person, particularly a man telling a woman what to do.

I was changing into someone that I didn't want to be, an angry and bitter person. I felt like I had lost control of my life and was constantly trying to please everyone else so that they would love me. There seemed to be a dark cloud hanging over me and no matter how hard I tried, it just kept getting darker. I didn't understand what was happening and I needed help. During those dark years I really hit rock bottom. I was in my late 30's and had already realized more than once that once you reach rock bottom, there was only one way to go - up! At least that was where I wanted to go, but I had no idea how to get there.

Then one day a friend took me to see psychic Sylvia Brown. Just spending a couple of hours listening to her helped me to understand what life was really all about. I realized that God had not forsaken me, rather I had turned away from him and no matter what mistakes I had made, he loved me unconditionally. That was a turning point in my life.

I was still struggling, but I wasn't feeling alone anymore. I had re-ignited a faith in God that I had somehow lost along the way. I was enjoying a spiritual journey and focusing on finding my own true path. Instead of dreading each day, I woke up feeling free and looking forward to the adventures awaiting me. Even the challenges that I still faced had become opportunities for me to grow and I welcomed them.

Along the path, I read many self-help books, but most were written by professionals using words that most of the people I knew, who really needed the help, had trouble understanding. I realized there was a need for a book about incest and sexual abuse written by someone these people could relate too. I wanted to help other women like me, their children and even hopefully reach the abusers themselves to encourage them to get help and stop the endless pain.

My most shocking revelation during my healing years was finding out just how complicated and deep the reaches of incest could be. I thought I was the only one in my family that it happened to. Was I ever wrong about that! I hope that by telling my story, I will be able to help others with their healing.

If, while reading it, something resonates with you, please pay attention to it. Whether it stirs up emotion because of a personal experience, or of someone that you know, it is your body telling you that there is a message here that you need to listen to. If you don't understand it now, perhaps you will by the end of my story.

If nothing else, I hope you enjoy reading it.

Fictional names have been used to protect others privacy.

CHAPTER ONE

1991

Despair

I survived the long drive home with my common-law husband Jeff, but I was still very angry at his behavior when we had been in Atlanta. I was sick of him bringing up my past and judging me for relationships that I had before I even met him. I kept telling him that what happened in my past was none of his business and not open for discussion, especially when he wasn't asking questions so that he could understand me better. I had made the mistake of sharing parts of my past with him in an effort to help him understand me.

I discovered later that his only interest was to have something to throw up in my face when we argued. I was anxious to end the relationship and either be on my own or find a man who really loved me just the way I was. I wanted a man that cared just as much about me being happy as he did about himself. Someone who would love and protect me, not someone that I needed protection from.

Shortly after our return from Atlanta we were watching TV one evening when we heard a crash, like breaking glass, and ran upstairs to find my six-year old daughter Jennifer and her bed covered in glass. The wind had apparently blown the window off its tracks and as it fell inward it must have hit her dresser and shattered all over the bed. She was crying, so I told her not to move until I could remove some of the glass and lift her off the bed. We managed to get the mess cleaned up quickly and Jen had just a couple of small scratches, but the thought of how much worse it could have been horrified me. I decided then that it was time to move out of that house and once again began looking for a new place to live.

I had kept in touch with my sister in-law Linda since my niece Sharon had been born the previous winter, in the hopes that I would be able to see Sharon grow up. Linda and my brother Bruce were having problems and if they broke up I didn't want to lose touch with Sharon as I had with my other nieces and nephew John. When I told Linda that I was looking for a place to live, she said that there was a house for rent just down the street from them. I went to check it out.

As usual Jeff told me to go ahead and take care of finding a place that I liked and he would move there. I would rather have moved without him. What did I need him for? As far as I could see I was doing most of the work taking care of the family, so what was the point? He wasn't taking care of me, so why should I put up with his bullshit? It was probably because I didn't feel good about myself after all I had been through and was afraid that if I left him I would be alone forever. I had been to hell and back with him over the past six and a half years and I'd had more than enough of him. I wasn't quite sure how to manage getting rid of him without a major confrontation yet, but I would figure it out soon.

We went to see the house and it was great, so we put in an application. There were three bedrooms upstairs; a big eat-in kitchen with a bay window that let in lots of sunshine and a good sized living room with sliding glass doors that led to a fair sized backyard. The yard was fenced in and there was plenty of room for a vegetable garden beside the patio. On the stairway down to the basement there was a small washroom and the basement contained a cold storage room and a small room that I could use for sewing. It didn't have a window, but it would be the perfect place for me to hide away from Jeff and just be myself.

The largest area of the basement was carpeted and had a brick fireplace, so Jeff and I would use that as our bedroom. Since we only had my three kids, Susan, Arthur and Jen living with us then, it would give the kids plenty of room upstairs. I loved it and hoped that our application would be accepted. The only down side for the kids was that the landlord didn't want any pets in the house, so we would have to get rid of our dog Harley. That was fine with me since Jeff and the kids had lost interest in taking care of him and that responsibility had fallen on me as well. I had enough to do working and looking after all the humans in the house, so the dog had to go.

Our application was accepted and when we moved we gave Harley to a friend of Jeff's who lived on a farm and had lots of room for him to run around. We could have gone to visit him anytime we wanted, but just as I suspected, we never did. Once he was gone everyone else seemed to forget about him. The kids didn't even mention going to see him, so I didn't either.

Once we got settled in we had a combination house-warming/Halloween party and I insisted that everyone attend in costume. We had a contest for the best costume, to be decided by a secret ballot. We had great fun and some of the costumes were outrageous. Mom came as a Las Vegas showgirl in a costume I had made for one of my lingerie meetings (a promotional meeting), Linda was a hippie and I was a leopard.

I had made a costume for myself from leopard print fabric and added black teddy and tights. My long hair was curled and tied up so that it surrounded my face and I had done my makeup the same as on the makeup package. At the end of the vote I won for best costume. As flattered as I was, I felt that as the hostess, the prize should go to the first runner-up, Mom.

I loved living in the house, but not with Jeff. It was great having Linda and her kids down the street, but I didn't see much of my brother Bruce. That was fine with me as we hadn't been very close over the past few years and he wasn't thrilled about me getting close to Linda. He had this thing about his family and didn't want much to do with us, saying that we were the cause of his problems. I thought it was more likely his alcohol problem that was ruining his life, but he didn't see that and had to blame somebody.

****

The Sewing Room

Christmas was only a couple of weeks away. I was very depressed and feeling the effects physically. I had turned the small room in the basement into my sewing room and I dreamt of the day that I would be able to have my own dressmaking business, creating custom clothing. Sewing and crafts had always helped me keep my sanity. I found sewing relaxing and it helped relieve my stress. But as the events of my life came and went, that tiny room without a window became so much more to me than just my sewing room. It became sacred - a place of my own. There I could breathe, allow myself just to be and temporarily escape my reality.

In that tiny room without a window, I spent hours sorting through the broken pieces of my life. With painstaking care I mended old rips, stitched up the tears and slowly sewed up the holes that had been left in my soul.

One day as I sat alone in my sewing room I was trying to understand why I always ended up with losers and why it was so hard to find a good man to share my life with. What was it about me that even my Daddy couldn't love me? What was I doing wrong that men treated me so badly? I started feeling like it was my fault that I couldn't have a healthy relationship and at times thought about just giving up. But where would that leave my three kids?

****

I had started to keep a journal in the hopes that by putting my feelings into writing I would be able to understand where I went wrong. All I wanted was a man to love that loved me back and treated me with the respect that I gave to him. I was thirty-three years old, feeling alone, hurt and very angry. All I wanted was a happy family and a comfortable home, which I thought was a reasonable expectation for someone who put everyone else's happiness above her own. It was time for me to re-examine my life and find some peace of mind if I was ever to be happy, something I didn't see any time in my future. I tried to have faith in God, asking for help to find a reason to go on.

I was having horrifying nightmares as well as serious pains in my stomach and groin and there were days that I could hardly move. After about a month I decided that I should go to a doctor. I didn't have much faith in doctors and thought most of them were quacks after what had happened to Mom, drugging her instead of finding out that she had a kidney stone. I had no alternative right now. There was definitely something wrong with my body and I couldn't function normally. When I looked back over the last few years I wasn't really surprised, so I decided to get help. As I wrote in my journal it stirred up a lot of unhappy feelings and at times I was afraid to continue writing. When the pain in my groin became unbearable, I finally went to my doctor and his diagnosis was Irritable Bowel Syndrome, which he said was caused by stress. His solution was some little white pills that would settle my bowel temporarily, but I would have to reduce the stress in my life. That sounded like a great idea, but how to achieve it? I told him I thought I should see a psychiatrist and he said he would set up an appointment for me.

Right after New Year's, only five days into 1992 my kids all came down with chicken pox. They spent the next two weeks home from school, scratching and complaining. Susan had it the worst and was pretty calm, but the other two were "full of beans" as Grandma used to say. Trying to keep the three of them from scratching off their scabs was a full time job and I thought I would go crazy.

I was still waiting to hear from my doctor about setting up an appointment with a psychiatrist, as I needed professional help to deal with all the stress. Gary, my CAS child management worker, had told me that my youngest child Jen had a need to make everyone around her anxious in order for her to feel comfortable and she was doing a great job of that. I was climbing the walls.

Jeff worked as a driver/salesman for Weston Bakeries, so he usually got home from work at around 10 a.m. every day. I would make sure I was busy with some project when he arrived as an excuse to stay down in my sewing room until the kids came home from school. He would usually call me upstairs to smoke a joint with him shortly after he got home, then I would go back downstairs and spend the rest of the day alone, while he sat upstairs watching TV.

That day after we had smoked a joint, I went back down to my sewing room and decided to do some writing instead of sewing. I loved to write and according to my English teachers, I appeared to be quite good at it. I believed that was because when I wrote it came from the heart, rather than from the head. I sat there alone in that room and wrote a poem that came straight from my heart, tears streaming down my cheeks. My tears were for the writer, in extraordinary pain, unable to function anymore day to day. I felt the hopelessness of a lost soul as I wrote on through my tears …

****

Does anyone hear the cries of the children, alone and afraid in the dark?

Maybe they hear, but are too afraid, to look into their own hearts.

"Ignore them," they say, "these children of ours, who we love and care for so dearly".

10

Then why don't they hear as we cry from our pain, when we can see it so clearly.

Our memories fade as we grow in our bodies, memories of pain and abuse.

But the child stays inside and never grows up, wondering, "What is the use?"

With nowhere to turn for love, warmth and caring, this pain that we bear may fade with sharing.

Childhoods lost in the depths of our minds, and experiences we can't remember.

When did we go wrong, January, May or December?

What did we do to these people we love, to make them ignore us, not see our pain?

They leave us or hurt us with actions and words, again and again and again.

Well the children grow up and being adult is hard, when inside a child's heart you see.

For whatever it was that made us so bad, is a mystery to you and to me.

We try so hard to be everyone's friend, to help them whatever they need.

But no matter how hard we try and try, there is no way that we can succeed.

For we're wounded and maimed by something we've done, way back when we were small.

But he's okay, they comfort him, so guess we must be the ones.

For they let him abuse us, this man they protect.

So we're bad and that is a fact, and the way we act when we cry out,

"is no way for a lady to act".

"Just forgive and forget", they tell us to do, "you're grown up and you are okay,

go on with your life and you will be fine, then abused yet another day".

They don't understand we don't have a life, for someone took it away.

The child was killed by this man that they know, but in the family he'll stay.

He left in her place this adult you see, with no hopes or dreams, just fears.

She cries all alone, for that's how it is, alone with her pain through the years.

Her mother's too busy with menial chores, or just too scared to see, that she's got wounds too, just like me.

Her brothers abuse her and tell her she's bad, she's a slut and a tramp and a sleaze.

"She's always been bad, this sister of ours, we're surprised she's not diseased".

For they're in pain too, but are too blind to see, that they're children inside, who have been hurt and by facing it they can be free.

To love and to grow as healthy men and stop the pain and abuse.

So alone she still cries and wonders why, and again, "what is the use?"

But somebody hears as she cries in her bed, the Lord up above in the sky.

She longs to be with him, where she can be safe, but to do that she must die.

Her time has not come to leave this world, full of pain, neglect and abuse.

For she hears the cries of the children, alone and afraid of the dark.

There's always a reason for the things we go through, the good, the bad and the ugly too.

We must help these children that nobody hears, and that's what she must now do.

When her life is over and her time has come, to be with her Lord in the sky.

She'll know that she did the best that she could, to see that no more children die!

****

When I finished writing, I read it over and cried my heart out. I couldn't believe that I had so much pain inside of me and prayed to God that somehow I could get rid of it. It was at times like these that I just wanted to jump in my car and drive it over a cliff or into a wall. I felt as though my whole family, the people who were supposed to love me and be there for me, had abandoned me. Like I wasn't worthwhile enough for even them to love me. My own father hadn't loved me enough to stick around.

If not for my own children and the fact that I was the only provider they had, I would have ended my life right then. Instead I looked at what would happen to my children if I were not there. My family would take care of them, the way they had taken care of me. Yes, they had been there for me as a child, giving me love, attention and the necessities of life, but understanding and support in a time of need were also necessities of life. Those things were important to me and I had tried to be there whenever any of my family needed me for emotional support.

When it came to relationships with men I felt stupid, lonely, hurt, angry and most of all confused. I had always thought of myself as a reasonably intelligent woman, so why did I keep ending up with needy, abusive men? Why couldn't I find a good man that just wanted to treat me as an equal, with love and respect? All I ever wanted was someone that I could share my life and my home with, to take care of each other. Why did I always have to be the one to take care of him? Who took care of me? I did, that's who.

****

Sex

I enjoyed sex as much as anyone else, but can't really say I ever had a man who really took care of me in that department. From my experiences, it was obvious that most men, at least the men I had been with were only interested in making sure they were taken care of. It didn't seem to matter much whether I was interested in having sex or not, it was at their demand. Most of the time I gave in, not wanting to cause any conflicts.

I just wanted a man who loved me just the way I was, not trying to change me and have me around for someone to have sex with every time he got a hard on. I could be very uninhibited as a lover, but when the man started treating me like that's all I was good at, I lost interest and it became a duty. And what if I didn't feel like it? I would do it anyway because it wasn't worth the confrontation if I didn't.

My ex-husband Max used to tell me that I had to have sex with him whenever he wanted because I was his wife. It was no different with Jeff. He would get cranky for days if I didn't have sex with him and once I gave in he would be happy again for a few days. Half the time neither of them even noticed that I wasn't enjoying it, as long as they were happy. I was just a warm body for them to get their rocks off with. It didn't matter if I wanted to or not.

It would be wonderful to be with a man who loved everything that I had to offer and could take "no" for an answer when it came to sex. There were times when I was

14

just too tired, or in pain, or just plain not in the mood. So why couldn't a man just understand that and not take it personally?

To me sex had become just a way to get what I wanted, whether it was to feel loved (even though I usually didn't), or just to get the man to leave me alone and stop pressuring me to do it. I was rarely able to enjoy sex just for the sake of enjoying it and maybe that was because I hadn't found a lover that only wanted it when we were both in the mood and cared if I reached orgasm too. Orgasm was pretty much a foreign word to me then. Female orgasm anyway-I was very familiar with the male orgasm.

****

I was not very pleased with my family at that time either. Mom was very skeptical about my getting counseling, thinking that the therapist would put ideas into my head. "Don't worry Mom", I thought, "there's enough going on in my head already." My family treated me like I was crazy or something, yet they were upset that I was in treatment. Isn't that what crazy people did? When I looked at them I could see just how dysfunctional my family was and none of them had any right to call me crazy. Both of my brothers were alcoholics and my parents did their fair share of indulging as well.

My brothers also went from relationship to relationship and both had children that they didn't see very often, if at all. So how was it that I was crazier than any of them? The only difference that I could see was that I recognized my problems and was attempting to do something about them. They were just whispering behind my back, "Droxy has problems".

Yes, I did have some problems and they could all be traced back to my family. There were many times that I was suicidal, but the thought of leaving my children for my family to raise made me reconsider. It was for my children that I fought to survive and overcome the damage done to me as a child and also to try and stop the circle of abuse.

There were many questions that I hoped I would be able to find answers to in the near future. I realized in that moment that before I could find a man that truly loved and respected me I would have to learn to love and respect myself first. I hoped that through my sessions with a therapist I would be able to do just that. Then maybe I could find some happiness.

CHAPTER TWO

1960's

The Family

My childhood was a happy one. I was lucky enough to grow up surrounded by a large, loving family. This was due mostly to the fact that my mother left my father George when I was only 4 years old and we ended up moving in with my maternal grandparents. They owned a beautiful bungalow in the suburbs, which was the perfect backdrop for many memorable childhood adventures. There were a lot of people in that house, so there was always something to do. First there was Grandma, who was always happy and loving while looking after all of us. Then there was Grandpa who was a minister. He made up the rules of the house and kept us all in line. Mom lived there too, working hard to support myself and my two younger brothers Bruce and Doug.

In addition to Mom and our family, also living there was Aunt Karen, who was more like a sister as she was only two years older than I. Then there was Aunt Lydia, who was crippled by Polio at a young age and needed our help. Uncle Doug, who was handsome and single, along with two or three foster children that Grandma and Grandpa took in at any time!

Grandma kept the house running smoothly with patience, understanding, laughter and lots of love for everyone. Holidays were a big celebration full of fun, great food, decorations and fancy clothes. Sometimes there were twenty or more people for Christmas dinner. Grandma would make name cards to put on the table so that everyone would know where to sit. That's what she told us anyway, but one day as I was helping her set the table, she told me that she really made them because she couldn't keep track of Uncle Doug's girlfriends. He was a very attractive young man and would have a different girlfriend on every occasion.

I loved helping Grandma set the table with her best dishes. She had a wonderful collection of different salt and pepper shakers and she used to tell me to pick out the ones that I wanted to use. I almost always picked the ones of Santa and Mrs. Claus. She knew that I admired her collection and told me that someday they would be mine.

Grandma was a great lady who made everyone around her feel special. She was always quick to smile and give out plenty of hugs and kisses. My favorite times were being with her in the kitchen when she was baking and cooking for the family. She made it all look so easy and was happy to teach me whatever she was doing. She taught me how to do crafts and I think it was her love of them that fueled my passion. If it wasn't for her patience in teaching me the things that I found difficult to learn, I don't know how I would have survived. Those crafts would carry me throughout my life, allowing me to make money to raise my children and hang on to my sanity when things got too tough.

Grandma would spend hours with the children, (at least those of us who were interested), sitting at the kitchen table making macaroni pictures. She would have different shapes of pasta, colored paper, sparkles, colored string, paint, glue - all the things that we needed to make beautiful works of art. When we were finished she would hang our artwork on the refrigerator or wall, wherever she could find room, so that the whole family could enjoy them. Most of the time the pasta ended up falling off onto the floor, but she would just replace the artwork with our next masterpiece.

I loved sitting beside her in the evening as she worked on a piece of lace or embroidery that she was doing. Back then, tablecloths, pillowcases, towels and placemats were hand embroidered, and Grandma decorated all of ours herself. She had beautiful patterns that were printed on tissue paper and she would iron them onto the fabric. Then she would use bright colors to embroider the pattern. When she was finished she would wash them and the ink from the pattern would disappear, leaving only the carefully embroidered picture. She used pictures that were mostly floral, or birds and butterflies. Even some that said "HIS" and "HERS".

My favorites were the pictures of Southern Belles in their big beautiful skirts. When I was about six years old Grandma told me that she would teach me how to embroider so that I could help her decorate our linens. She started me off with simple patterns of kittens and flowers and it wasn't long before I had moved onto the more complicated patterns. There were several different stitches to learn, most of them simple, but the one that took the longest to master was the French Knot. It was mostly used for eyes or the center of flowers, so I didn't have to do it often and even today I avoid using that stitch whenever possible.

Aunt Vicky, Grandma's twin sister, did needlework called petit point. It involved using canvas rather than fabric and the picture came out looking like a painting. It was very fine stitching and Grandma spent hours helping me learn how to do them evenly. I loved doing it, but later turned to needlepoint, which was done on a heavier canvas with yarn instead of embroidery floss.

Grandma bought me a kit that included everything I needed to create a picture. The pattern was a young girl in a pretty dress, holding flowers. When I had finished carefully stitching it, I got Mom to help me frame it and gave it back to Grandma for her birthday so that she could hang it on the wall. She cried when she opened it. She was so proud that I had done it without asking her for help.

Before she died she made sure that Mom gave it back to me to remind me of her. Like I needed anything to remind me of her! She was so special to me that I would remember everything about her forever. I kept the picture for many years, but when my daughter Susan moved to her own apartment I gave it to her.

Cross-stitch also became one of my favorite pastimes. It could be done on fabric or on special Aida cloth that had small squares, which made the stitching easier. The stitches were an X done over each square of the fabric. Like the petit point, from a distance the picture looked like a painting. Many years later someone gave me a software program as a gift, which allowed me to create my own patterns from any picture. I was able to use the program to make patterns for other people and earn some money from it.

Next Grandma taught me to crochet the lace edging for pillowcases. I remembered how hard it was to teach me with her being right handed and me being left handed. I couldn't hold the hook the same way that she did and had to use my right hand to hold it. I was finally able to figure out a way to hold it with the hook going under my hand instead of over my hand like Grandma held it. That made it harder for her, so she finally gave me an instruction book that had illustrations I could follow and practice while she was busy with her own work.

The first thing that I actually made was navy blue lace that Grandma later hand stitched onto two pillowcases. When I showed the finished cases to Mom, she was so proud that I decided that what I most wanted to do was create beautiful things to make them both proud. Mom was excited mostly because she didn't even know how to crochet. When I was a little older (and thought Mom was old enough) I taught her how to do it. I guess she figured if her little girl could do it, she should be able to learn as well. It was a bit of a challenge with the right and left handed thing, but I still had my instruction book from Grandma, so I had to let her figure some of it out herself.

She made a big beautiful white lace doily to put on one of the tables. It made me so proud of both of us that I had been able to teach my mother something. She already knew how to knit and made the most cozy baby sweater sets that she would later end up making for people who wanted them for shower gifts.

Grandma and Mom had a hard time teaching me to knit too, again because of them both being right handed and me left. Mom had been left handed when she was younger, but told me that when she went to school the teacher would tie her left hand behind her back so that she would have to learn how to write with her right hand. I thought that was so cruel and wondered why the teacher didn't want her to use her left hand to write. What possible difference could it make? Later when I was learning how to write in school, I would lose grades on my papers because I wrote with a left handed back slant, just as my mother had.

It was also Grandma who taught me the things that I would later need to know about taking care of a family. I don't remember ever hearing her raise her voice in anger, (unfortunately I didn't quite get the hang of that lesson), but many times she raised her voice in song (I did get that lesson). She used to sing or whistle (I never could do that) while she worked and you could just feel the joy radiating from her heart. I wanted to be just like her when I grew up. That didn't actually happen, although I did remember most of the lessons she taught me. I'm happy to say that I ended up with a lot of the inner qualities as both she and my mother.

Mom had a very difficult life and my life followed more in her footsteps than in Grandma's. In the times that she grew up, sex was not something that ladies talked about. My grandmother, being a lady, had never discussed such matters with my mother and at the age of sixteen, Mom became pregnant with me. According to her, she wasn't even sure how it happened.

When I was old enough to understand, she told me that my grandparents had considered adopting me at birth and raising me as their own. Instead, my mother and father got married, as was expected in those days. They got married on Valentine's Day, which at the time must have seemed very romantic, but as it turned out, it was not a match made in heaven. Her wedding pictures showed a lovely young bride and her handsome young husband, only a year older than she, smiling and looking very much in love.

Their marriage didn't last more than four years, during which time my father was in and out of jail several times. I never even cared enough to ask what for. During their short marriage they had two more children, Bruce who was two years younger than me and Doug who was four years younger. So by the age of twenty-one, Mom was divorced with three small children. She was too busy working to support us to have much time to spend with us. She had help from my grandparents and none from my father.

It was my grandmother who was there with us, doing the mothering that Mom was unable to do. When I was about eighteen, Mom came to me and apologized for having neglected me and I was shocked. I had never felt that she had neglected me. Both of my brothers played hockey on different teams and she took them both to practices and games. I guess that's why she felt I had been left out. But I used to go along to the games and watch all the NHL games on TV. That meant I missed a lot of shows that I wanted to watch, but when I was older I would come to appreciate all the things that my mother did for me.

Memories of my father are few and far between as he was not the kind of man who took responsibility for his children. He visited us for awhile, but used to drop us off at his parents' house while he went off with whomever he was dating at the time. When Mom found out, she stopped his visits. She didn't tell me that until many years later when I asked her specific questions about him.

While we were growing up she didn't say bad things to us about him, she answered our questions as honestly as she could, appropriate to our age. Even though she did her best to hide it, I could sense her bitterness towards him and sometimes thought it irrational, until I was in my teens. That's when I began to understand and share her distaste of him.

****

George

Although, I had never taken any real interest in my father before, when I turned sixteen, I decided to look him up. I'm not sure why, but I guess I was curious and thought it was time that we get to know each other better. He had never really been a part of my life and he hadn't been anything like a father was supposed to be like. I never called him Dad, just George. So I decided to visit George and called him up.

It was a great visit and he was happy to see me. A little too happy maybe! When I kissed him goodbye, he stuck his tongue in my mouth.

****

I never really got to know George's side of the family that well, so I don't remember very much about them. We didn't keep in touch over the years. I must have had some contact with them as a child however, because Mom had given me photos of his parents and I together. His grandparents lived in a small house between our house and our school, so I used to drop in to visit sometimes after school. What I remember most about them were the milk bottles. They had their milk delivered by a man in a dairy truck and I would bring them in whenever I came to visit or put the empty bottles out for pick up the next day.

I was very young when they died, so I didn't attend their funerals. George's grandfather (my great grandfather), as I was told, became senile and spent his last few years in a mental health facility (I thought of it as an "asylum" back then). That left an impression on me. When I was older and anyone would call me crazy I would freak out. I thought that maybe I might turn out like him – that it was hereditary. He eventually died there and I was devastated, as that was my first experience with the death of a loved one. Great Grandma died of natural causes in a nursing home, but I had no recollection of it.

Once their house was sold and Great Grandma had gone to the nursing home, I missed going to their house after school. Even though I hadn't gone every day, it had been comforting to know that they were there anytime I wanted to see them.

George's parents (my paternal grandparents) didn't bother visiting us, but every once and awhile they would drop off a gift for birthdays or Christmas. Mom wouldn't have objected to them spending time with us; they were God fearing people just like her parents.

Because I grew up without my biological father, my maternal grandfather was the only father I knew until I was thirteen. He looked so young that my friends all thought he was my father when they first saw him. He was a big man with a deep voice and he kept us in line just by showing his disapproval when we did something "wrong". Until the day he died the whole family was careful around him, because there was nothing worse than feeling Grandpa's disapproval.

He worked at a meat packing plant that was owned by Grandma's two brothers, and I always remembered the jingle that they used in their advertising. I would hear it on the radio and see commercials on TV. I knew that my grandma's family name was known by just about everybody who had a radio. I thought they must be famous. I also thought that Grandpa must have made pretty good money to be able to take care of all of us, although he did clip coupons. He was "reducing, recycling and re-using" long before it was popular. We just thought he was very thrifty.

My Aunt Lydia, who was crippled by polio when she was five or six years old could still walk, but her toes were turned inwards when she did, so she had a difficult time. She was only about four feet tall and because she couldn't bend her legs at the hips she was unable to put on socks or shoes easily. She would have to sit on the couch and put each leg up on it in order to reach her foot. From a very young age I learned that it was much easier for her with help, so I would help her whenever she needed to get dressed.

Every Sunday the family would dress in our "Sunday best" and go to church, where Grandpa was the minister and Aunt Lydia was my Sunday school teacher. It was a quaint little church with a small congregation, so everyone knew each other. We were more like an extended family than just neighbors. My favorite place in the church was the library. It was very small and dusty, but the shelves went all the way around from floor to ceiling and they were loaded with books. I loved to read and every week took several home with me.

I wanted to know everything there was to learn in that room and go to all the exotic places there were to go. There was a hidden passageway behind some of the shelves with stairs leading up to the main floor. I used to love sneaking in there just to sit quietly and read a book, or go up the stairs to see what the adults were doing in the chapel.

Sometimes Grandpa would ask me to sing for the adults and I felt so special to be invited upstairs (Sunday school for the children was in the basement). I would practice all week and was always a little nervous when I first got up on stage, but once I started singing all I cared about was making sure everyone in the back pews could hear me. After the service, almost everyone would come over to me and say how much they had enjoyed my singing.

When I was about twelve or thirteen, Grandpa baptized me in a small pool that was covered by floorboards off the stage. He explained the ceremony to me and made sure that I understood that by participating I was dedicating my life to God. I loved God and the whole thing sounded wonderful to me. I had faith that if I lived by his word - the Bible, he would always love me back. I knew that Grandpa was proud of me too and that was very important to me.

He was a good man who had devoted his life to God. That turned out to be a good thing for him as he almost died a couple of times and I'm sure it was God who came to his rescue. I was too young to remember the first time, but he was backing out of the driveway in a small car when a bigger car came speeding down the street and broadsided him. He was thrown over to the other side of the car and his neck was broken. Somebody was sure looking out for him that day as not too many people survive a broken neck. Grandpa did and once he recovered he was healthy and showed no signs of permanent damage. Many years later he would survive another serious car accident and broken neck. It was truly a miracle.

Most Sundays after church, Grandma would take the children to visit her mother. Great Grandma's house always smelled of mothballs and I still think of her every time I smell them. She was very tall and Grandma told me that when she and her twin sister Vicky were babies, Great Grandma had to carry them around on a cushion so that they wouldn't slip through her arms. They were only about one pound each when they were born and Great Grandma told me that she could slip her wedding ring almost all the way up their arms. Even though I loved her very much I didn't look forward to visiting her. I didn't know why, I adored her little house with lace doilies on the tables and I used to sit beside her on the bench while she played the piano for us.

After she played the piano she always brought out a fancy tin of candies and we were all allowed to have just one, unless the rules changed and then it was just two. When she died after a long battle with cancer (and she never smoked even one cigarette), I was very upset for a long time.

Hers was the first funeral I attended and I couldn't even cry until she was taken to the cemetery for burial. All I wanted was to turn back the clock. I promised God that if he brought her back I would always look forward to Sundays at her house. I thought that if I was really good I could make a bargain with God. When my prayers didn't come true, I thought I had displeased God and he didn't love me anymore.

I didn't know anything about my maternal grandfather's family. It wasn't something he talked about. From what I could gather from bits and pieces of conversation (accidentally overheard, of course), his parents died before I was born. He had one brother and apparently they didn't get along. I thought that was strange, Grandpa being a minister and all. I thought ministers were supposed to get along with everyone, especially their own family. But I guess he must have had his own reasons.

Besides the bungalow, my grandparents also had a cottage up north and that's where we spent our summers. Grandma would take the kids up there the day after school was out and we would stay the whole summer until school started again. I always enjoyed the drive there and back. The closest town was Minden and we always stopped at the Kawartha Dairy in town for some ice cream. They had the best ice cream in the world and many different flavors (at least ten!).

Grandpa came up on the weekends and took us skiing, boating, fishing, etc. I enjoyed those activities, but the fact that we weren't allowed to do any of them on Sundays was a drag. On Sundays we weren't allowed to play board games, read comic books or watch TV, except for Billy Graham or other religious shows. We could do it during the week, except for playing cards. There was never a time we were allowed to play cards - they were for gambling and therefore bad.

I really missed Mom during the summers as she had to stay in the city and work, but she would come up as often as she could and spent her vacations with us. We were kept very busy having fun, so the time in between went quickly.

The cottage was in a small cove on Halls Lake, which was crystal clear with a clean, sandy bottom - not the kind that made the water muddy when we swam. Grandma used to tell me I was like a little mermaid as she had a hard time getting me to come out of the water. I was a very strong swimmer and loved to spend as much time in the water as I could.

The summer I remember most at the cottage, was when Aunt Karen had a boyfriend for the first time. I was eleven then and her boyfriend's sister Sherri was about the same age, so we hung out together.

One day Karen and her boyfriend John were going for a romantic walk along the road and Sherri and I decided to follow and spy on them, to see if they were kissing or something. A car was driving down the road and we suddenly realized that if Karen or John turned around to look at it, they would be able to see us in the headlights. We panicked and dove into the bushes beside the road.

When I hit the ground I got a blinding pain in my left knee and let out a scream. That blew our cover of course, but I didn't care, it hurt really badly. I was able to stand up and limp out onto the road and I could feel that my pants were wet. It was too dark to see anything, so Sherri and John helped me hobble over to the light at the front of their cottage.

We saw to our horror that my pant leg was soaked with blood. Karen freaked out and ran to our cottage to get Grandma while John helped me make my way slowly back. It didn't hurt much after a couple of minutes. It had gone numb, so I didn't think it was too serious an injury - just slap a Band-Aid on it and I'd be fine. WRONG!

Finally, we got to the cottage where Grandma was and luckily she had worked as a registered nurse, so she knew what to do. She remained calm while assuring me that she would have it cleaned and bandaged in no time. I knew that she would draw a happy face with Mercurochrome just to make me smile. Grandma could fix most anything, with love in her heart and a smile on her face, never cross or impatient.

This time she wouldn't be able to fix it. When she cut open my pant leg all we could see was a big hole in my leg, right under my knee and it was full of blood. I cried and screamed when I realized that the closest hospital was just over twenty miles away! Fortunately some friends of our family were there and they had a station wagon they could use to transport me. They put an air mattress in the back for me to lie on and their daughter Megan lay down beside me to keep me company.

It turned out that I must have landed on a piece of glass and it had gone in very deep. The doctor had to put three stitches on the inside, six on the outside and a big bandage around it. That was pretty much the end of my fun that summer. I couldn't walk or swim very well and ended up spending most of my time in bed or on the couch in the living room.

I was very upset and kept telling Grandma that all I wanted was my mother, but she had to work and couldn't come up until the weekend. I was so glad to see her just because she was Mom. She really couldn't do anything that Grandma wasn't doing, but just having her there made everything better. As I grew older I would dearly miss those summers at the cottage.

Looking back, these were the things I remembered and treasured. My childhood was fun, filled with laughter, lots of things to do and most importantly, so many incredible family members to spend time with. I felt very loved and secure.

So I didn't understand why later in life, I slipped into such darkness or why I felt so lonely and empty all the time. I didn't understand why I had this feeling of not being worthy of love, nor did I see a reason for the rage that boiled up inside me. I especially didn't understand why it was so hard to find a good man that loved me and cared for me. The darkness was the biggest mystery to me. It was something that grew stronger as I got older, especially as I struggled to carve out a life of my own, a family of my own and a love of my own.

CHAPTER THREE

1986

A Life of My Own

I was living in a house with my children and two boarders because I couldn't afford the house on my own. My daughter Susan was 7, my son Arthur was 2 and my youngest daughter Jennifer was just over 1. There was one boarder living in the basement named Justin. He had been a Vagabond biker in his younger years, but at the time worked as the General Manager of a trucking company. He was so big that his nickname was Bear, but he was very gentle and looked out for all of us. The boarder living upstairs was named Katy. She was a college student that dressed like a punk rocker. Again, she wasn't at all as she appeared to be, with her platinum blonde hair spiked and tipped with black. She was very intelligent and lots of fun to have around.

One day Justin brought a young girl home named Emma and asked me if she could stay for a while. He didn't have a romantic interest in her, she was only twenty years old and he was in his late forties, but she had no place to stay and he wanted to help her out. I told him that she could stay for a short period, but he would have to find her somewhere else to go. Justin had recently started dating a friend of mine from work and they were getting serious, so he spent most of his time at her place and Emma was left to entertain herself. She hung out at the house with us a lot and we liked her fine, but she was a very disturbed girl. Her boyfriend was in jail, so she was having a hard time dealing with life. I could relate to how she was feeling, but I had my own pain to deal with and I was drinking too much again, trying to maintain my sanity.

One afternoon, my brothers Bruce and Doug were over having a few beers and Emma joined us. She went downstairs after awhile and we thought she had gone down to have a nap or something. In the meantime, Bruce and Doug's wives had called several times asking if their husbands were there, but both my brothers begged me not to tell them. I didn't see the sense of it, since I figured it must be okay for Bruce and Doug to visit with their own sister, but apparently not.

After a few calls, I told Bruce and Doug that if either of their wives called again I was not lying for them anymore. They would have to talk to them or I was going to be the bad guy when they found out the truth and that wasn't fair.

I was in the process of doing laundry and had to check on it in the basement, so I was very quiet not to disturb Emma. When I went down the stairs I couldn't believe what I saw. Emma was lying across the bed unconscious and both of her wrists were cut and bleeding. I ran back up the stairs and yelled for someone to call 911 and get an ambulance on the way. I grabbed a couple of cloths, wet them and ran back down to tend to Emma until the ambulance came. I wasn't sure what to do, but common sense told me that the first thing was to wrap the cloths around her wrists to try and stop the bleeding as much as possible. Bruce came down with me to check and see if she was still alive while Doug called 911. She was alive and when I looked at her wrists more closely, they weren't bleeding too badly. The cuts she had made were not very deep. Hopefully they weren't deep enough for her to bleed to death. It didn't look like she had lost much blood yet, so we were optimistic. The ambulance finally arrived and Bruce said that he was going to the hospital with her and I would follow shortly in my car. Katy and Doug said they would stay with the kids, so I went to change my clothes and headed to the hospital.

When I got there I found Bruce waiting outside her room. He told me that the paramedics had said that the injuries weren't serious and it looked more like a cry for help than a suicide attempt. I was thankful for that and felt great sadness for her as she was so young and I could relate to feeling so lost and hopeless. Two police officers came out of her room and started asking me about her and what had happened. I didn't have much to tell them as she had only been at my house for two weeks and all I really knew about her was that her boyfriend was in jail. I didn't know of any family or where she had been before coming to my place.

As I was talking to the police officers, the door at the end of the hallway swung open and Deirdre and Stella, (my brother's wives) walked through them and headed straight for me. They were calling me names and freaking out because I had lied to them. Fortunately, the officers got them under control immediately and asked both of them to leave. I was relieved that they were gone and Bruce went with them. I had enough to deal with without two irate wives yelling at me.

When I called Bruce's wife Deirdre later, I told her that she had no right to yell at me as I hadn't told her anything. I hadn't even spoken to her, Katy had. She apologized for her attack at the hospital and agreed that she had no right to be angry with me even if I had lied to her. Bruce was my brother after all and she would probably have done the same thing if put on the spot like that. We were okay, but Doug's wife Stella wouldn't take my calls and strangely enough, Doug didn't return my calls either. I didn't know why he was angry with me, but apparently he was.

Emma came back to the house the next day and I told Justin that he had better try to find somewhere else for her to stay. I had kids who were having a hard time dealing with my problems, without having some stranger trying to kill herself in our basement. He agreed and said that he would get right on it. I liked Emma and felt bad for her, but I had to take care of my family first.

The next thing I knew, she came home with a guy named Jeff that she had met at a bar. He was my age and about my height, with short blonde hair, mustache and beautiful blue eyes. She brought him home because he had a fight with his wife in front of some guests who were at his home. His wife had kicked him out and he was going to get a motel room, but had driven Emma home first as it was too far for her to get home by cab. We talked for awhile and he seemed to be a nice enough guy.

He explained that his wife was manic-depressive and was having a few bad days. They hadn't been getting along for a few years and he was tired of it, especially when he caught her in bed with some guy that night. I felt bad for him too, but again, I had my own baggage to deal with. I went to bed and left Emma to say goodnight to her new friend. I was planning my birthday party in a few days and told Emma that if she wanted to, she could invite Jeff. He could keep her company, as she wouldn't know very many people at the party.

For the next few days I was busy with party plans. I hadn't had a party in a long time and I wanted to make sure everyone had a good time. Emma's new friend Jeff had been spending quite a bit of time at our house and had apparently been loaning her his car while he was at work. He seemed perplexed at the mileage she was putting on it and found out that she had been using it to go up north to visit her boyfriend in jail. He had also been giving her money to pay me rent and he was beginning to get the idea that maybe she was just using him for money and transportation.

They weren't sleeping together as she was very young and he was about twelve years older. He didn't want to get into that kind of relationship with her. They were just hanging out and trying to help each other deal with the crap they were going through and had become good friends. I didn't realize at the time that he was spending so much time at the house because he wanted to get to know me.

I kind of had a feeling, as most of the time he was there he would talk to me, following me around. I wasn't really surprised when he asked me out for dinner one night and I didn't see why I shouldn't go out with him. He seemed okay and was only a couple of years older than I was. At the time, I was a few months into getting over my latest boyfriend, Carter. I was keeping busy and trying not to think about him, just focusing on work and the kids, making a nice home for them. Jeff and I went out on our dinner date a few days later and had a very nice time. He was a perfect gentleman, a quality I had only seen in a boyfriend once before.

Emma hadn't invited Jeff to the party, so I asked him to come as my date. It was a great success and everyone enjoyed themselves for the most part. My ex-brother-in-law Wade and his wife Nancy came and were already well on their way to being drunk when they arrived. They ended up having a big fight, but that was apparently the tone of their entire marriage, then and for years to come.

My best friend Kevin and his wife Kathy were pretty much the same. They didn't seem to get along at all and I wasn't the only one wondering what he was doing with her. He was such a warm and happy person and she was just the opposite. There were times I would be having a conversation with her and she was sweet as pie one minute, then it was like someone hit a switch and she didn't have anything nice to say about anything. I would politely excuse myself and move on to someone else who was having fun. At least Kevin didn't let her spoil his good time. He just ignored her as much as possible and mingled with everyone else.

Jeff did come as my date for the evening and everyone seemed to like him, which I saw as a good sign. They were the people who I thought knew me and they thought he would be good for me. He ended up spending the night and within a month had moved in with us. Justin was planning to move out to live with his girlfriend Liz, so the timing was great. My rent would stay the same as Jeff would take over paying Justin's third when he moved out. That was the beginning of our six-year relationship.

CHAPTER FOUR

1986

Jeff

It was about four months after Jeff moved in that his wife Penny decided that he could bring his kids to the house for a visit. I wasn't aware at the time that she understood him to be renting a room in my house, rather than living with me as my boyfriend. I wasn't comfortable being affectionate with him around his kids anyway, until they got to know me better. I figured he was probably thinking the same thing. He had a stepdaughter named Teresa who was 12, a daughter Jane who was 7 and his son Brian was 5. They were all adorable and we got along great.

It wasn't long before little Brian developed a crush on me and told Jeff that he thought his landlady was pretty. That was my first clue that Jeff had lied to Penny about our situation. When I asked Jeff what he had told her, he said that he didn't tell her I was his girlfriend, as he was afraid she wouldn't let him see the kids. He just needed me to be patient for a little while and then he would tell her. He seemed to think that I would leave him because of it and begged me to just stand by him and be patient. Sometimes it got to the point of him pleading, "Please don't ever leave me, I can't live without you". I didn't have a problem giving him some time to work things out as they were newly separated and hadn't been to court yet. Then there was the fact that she was mentally unstable and had spent much of their marriage in the hospital psychiatric ward.

When it came time for Justin to move out, Jeff said that he wanted to use the basement as our bedroom instead of staying in the small room upstairs. He was hoping that my other boarder Katy would decide to move out soon as well, so that we could have the whole house to ourselves. He liked her fine, but he earned good money and wanted to be a family, so we didn't need the extra money that she paid for rent.

Jeff arranged for his kids to come and visit for Christmas and we bought all the kids a mountain of presents. I had bought Jeff a diamond ring for Christmas. I hoped that one day we would get married and be just one big, happy family. I couldn't wait to see his face when he opened it. We were really looking forward to having his kids over and being able to celebrate with them too. By then Jeff had told his children that I was his girlfriend because they had started asking questions. I had no problem lying to Penny, but I wasn't going to lie to the kids. The adults would just have to deal with the situation the same as I had to.

The day before Christmas, Penny called to tell Jeff that she had checked herself into the psychiatric ward at the hospital again and that the children were in the care of the Children's Aid Society. He was furious. We couldn't understand why she hadn't just called him. We would have taken them to our house. I figured she was having a hard time during the holidays and felt she needed to go to the hospital. That was fine, but it wasn't fair to the kids or Jeff to put them into foster care when they could have stayed with us. I could only assume that Penny was jealous and would rather have them spend the holidays with strangers than with their father and his new family. I couldn't believe how selfish and petty some people could be.

Naturally it was impossible to find out where they were as Penny said she didn't know and the CAS office wasn't answering the phone. We could only hope that the kids would call us, but they didn't. It turned out to be a very depressing holiday, although we tried to make the best of it with my kids.

The highlight for both Jeff and I was when he opened the diamond ring. I told him that I hoped someday, when he had sorted out his current marital situation and was free, we would get married. He had tears in his eyes when he told me that he hoped for the same.

Shortly after New Year's, Katy told me she was moving out. She loved living with us, but felt like a third wheel and she had heard Jeff and I talking about the possibility of his kids staying with us for a while. I didn't want her to leave, but Jeff was ecstatic. He would get what he wanted.

Just after Christmas, Jeff finally reached CAS and was trying to get temporary custody of his kids while Penny was in the hospital. Apparently, she had made up some story about him not caring about the kids, which was why CAS had not contacted him. They weren't aware that he had any interest in taking care of the kids. Now he had to fight CAS just to be able to talk to them.

The children were finally able to call him, but were not allowed to tell him where they were. Penny was obviously trying to get him back as she probably realized that without him she was going to have to take care of the kids by herself. She had met a couple in the hospital and given them the keys to the house, letting them stay there until she got out and Jeff was not happy about it.

The house was a rental, but all of his possessions, other than his clothes, were still there. He didn't have a problem letting Penny keep whatever furnishings she needed when she had the kids, but he wasn't about to leave everything for strangers to do what they wanted with. His solution was to move back into the house himself and kick them out, which he did. He told me that Penny wasn't living there and he was only staying until he could get her and the children home again. Then he would be back. I didn't see that I had a choice as my roommates were now gone and he was the only one helping me pay the rent at the house.

The day after Jeff went back to his house I had a strange feeling in the pit of my stomach. I didn't know why, but something told me that he was at the hospital with Penny, so I went there. I was sitting in my car in the parking lot thinking how foolish I was. Why would he be there and why at that time of day? Then I looked up and what did I see? Jeff and Penny walking towards his car, hand in hand.

I pulled my car up in front of his and just sat there until he saw me. He helped Penny into his car and walked over to me. I couldn't believe the look on his face. He didn't look anything like the man that I loved. His eyes were the coldest I had ever seen before, or since - and I was devastated. It was like he didn't even recognize me. I couldn't believe that he was the same man who for the past several months had been telling me how much he loved me and begging me not to leave him. I simply said, "I want my ring back". He reached for it, took it off his finger and handed it to me without a word. Then he turned around and walked back to his car. I looked down at it and my heart ached. I had bought him that ring only two months before and I was amazed that things could have changed so much in his heart in so short a time. I had thought things between us were great, but I was obviously wrong.

For the next two days I couldn't eat or sleep and did nothing but walk around the house crying. I finally realized that I had to pull myself together for the kids. They were beginning to get upset and it was hard for them too. They had become attached to Jeff and he was like their father.

The following night I was watching TV, when I noticed a car pull up in front of the house. The headlights were on and it was just sitting there, so I went to the window to see if it was someone that I knew. It was Jeff, so I went outside to see what he wanted and why he was there. He was very drunk and when I got into the car I turned it off and took the keys. Even if I was mad at him I wasn't going to let him drive any further in that condition. I was surprised he had made it that far. He was crying and started telling me that he had packed up his clothes and left, he couldn't stay with Penny. He didn't love her and hadn't for years. He said that he had only gone back to try and get his kids back home, then planned on suing her for custody as he would have no problem proving she was an unfit mother.

He went on to say that he was in love with me and couldn't live without me. He told me that when he thought he had lost me, he was going to go and drive his car into a tree and just end it. He sounded like he really meant to hurt himself, so I convinced him to come into the house and sleep it off so we could talk about it in the morning. I wasn't about to take him into my bed again so easily, so I put him on the couch and gave him a blanket. He was so drunk I don't think he even realized where he was and I was anxious to see how he felt about things in the morning when he sobered up.

The following morning when I got up, Jeff was already up. He had made coffee and was working on breakfast, making himself right at home. It was nice of him to make the effort, but I wasn't in the mood for breakfast and it was going to take a lot more than that to get back on my good side. We sat down over coffee and he repeated what he had told me the night before.

He wasn't suicidal anymore and practically begged me to give him another chance. He was going to wait for Penny to get the kids out of CAS care herself, then file for divorce and sue for custody. He needed my support if he was going to get that, as he wanted to live with both his kids and I. I told him I would give it some thought, but that he could stay at the house for the time being and sleep on the couch. I would have to see how things went before I trusted him again.

A week or so later, my ex-husband Max, was at the house visiting the kids. Jeff called and said that Penny had just called him to say that she was being evicted from the house and didn't know what to do. He was concerned about the furnishings and asked if I would call a rental company to reserve a truck for that evening and he would pick it up on his way home. He would need a storage space for the furniture, so asked if I would call and arrange that too and he would pay for it. I said that I would and Max said that he would go with me to the storage place and help me out.

I couldn't imagine why Max offered, as he was useless and I was capable of renting a storage space myself. I'd had to do it when I left him. I didn't feel like arguing, so I told him he could come along. I went over and made the arrangements, getting back before our seven-year-old daughter Susan got home from school. Max visited with Susan for a few minutes, then finally left.

When Jeff got home with the truck, he had brought a couple of buddies with him to help out, so as soon as they arrived we all got in the truck and went to pick up his things. Penny was alone when we got there and obviously drinking. I had brought some boxes with us and started packing stuff up right away as she hadn't packed anything and there was a lot to do in a short time. The men were loading things on the truck and Penny was just standing around with a drink in her hand. There were only three men, so it was taking too long to get the big furniture out. I decided to help with that and not bother with the packing. I thought if Penny wanted the dishes and things she could get off her lazy ass and pack them herself. Jeff was more concerned about the larger items anyway. I was helping carry the dressers and beds downstairs and I guess Penny finally got the idea that perhaps she could help, so she started carrying out the lamps and smaller furniture pieces.

As soon as we had it all on the truck, we left. Penny was supposed to be getting picked up by her new boyfriend to go to his place. I had to get home and take care of my kids as the babysitter had to be home by eleven p.m., so I left the men to put the stuff into the storage unit. It was very late by the time they finished and Jeff got home. At least all his household furnishings were safely stored for the time being and he told Penny that when she found an apartment she could pick them up. I had a house full of furniture that I had bought since I left Max, so we really didn't need any of it and she would need it when she got the kids back.

****

Men

I wasn't sure exactly when I had stopped trusting men, but when I thought back over my life, what man had I been able to trust? Certainly not my father George, he had left me when I was only 4 years old. It seemed that I would fall in love with a man and let him take control of my life. It wasn't that I wasn't perfectly capable of taking care of myself, but for some reason when it came to men, I always felt that they were in control of me. As long as I did what they wanted, and became the person that they wanted me to be, they wouldn't leave. I found myself living a life that wasn't true to me, but I wasn't complete without a man, so I had to do whatever it took to keep him.

****

CHAPTER FIVE

1987

Betrayed

Jeff and I had been getting along okay since he had come back to the house and things had settled down between us. He wanted me to quit my job and let him take care of us. I was having problems at work anyway, so I would have loved to quit, but I wanted to have my own money. One day while I was at work I started feeling really sick. I told my boss Albert and he could see how sick I was, but he had nobody to cover my shift, so I had to finish working it myself.

That night I was up vomiting and running a fever, so I called Albert early in the morning and told him that I wouldn't be able to work that day. He told me that even though he knew that I was sick, he would need me to get a note from my doctor. I couldn't believe that he actually expected me to take my three kids and go to the doctor for a note, especially when he knew that I was sick. I didn't have a car, and I wasn't about to take them all to the doctor on the bus. It wasn't like I would get paid for the day if I got a note. I told him that he could shove his job up his ass and I quit.

Jeff was very happy when I told him, but I told him that I was going to look for something else even if it was only part-time. I got the feeling that he was trying to make me dependent on him so that I would never leave him. I had told him right at the start of our relationship not to ever think that I was so dependent on him that I wouldn't leave. I had learned that lesson from previous relationships, but I guess he thought that would change if he were supporting the kids and I. I also didn't want to be at home with nobody except the kids to talk to all day. I liked being in the work force. Because of my past experiences with men, it was also important that I knew I could take care of myself without them. That way I didn't have to stay in a relationship if it turned out the same way the rest of them had.

A few days later, Jeff's friends Roy and Bonnie came over for a visit. While Roy and Jeff went out to get beer, Bonnie and I caught up. Bonnie told me about a friend of hers who just found out that her boyfriend of five years had been cheating on her. I said that one thing I loved about Jeff was that I never had to worry about him cheating on me. I had grown to trust him and knew that I could. She looked very uncomfortable and I asked her what was wrong. She told me that she really hated to be the one to tell me, but considered me her friend and thought I had the right to know that Jeff had cheated on me. She wouldn't tell me with whom and said that I would have to ask Jeff if I wanted the details. I was devastated. I had been so sure that he was faithful.

As soon as Roy and Jeff returned from their beer run, Bonnie took Roy aside and they left shortly after. I guess she knew that I was no longer in the mood for company and needed to have a serious discussion with Jeff. As soon as they left, I confronted Jeff. He admitted that he had been at a local strip club and had gone up to one of the rooms with a twenty-year-old stripper and had sex with her. I asked him if that was the only time.

He told me that he had also continued to meet with Penny a few months before and that once or twice she had followed him to the washroom at the bar, where she had been giving him blow jobs. He said that he hadn't seen her for a long time and that he had only been meeting her then because he was trying to get her to help him get the kids out of CAS and into his custody. He said that he was ashamed of himself as he really did love me, but he knew that he had screwed up and would move out by the weekend.

45

There was no way I was letting him off the hook that easily and told him that he was not moving out. I wanted him to stay and pay for his mistakes. He had convinced me to let my roommates move out, quit my job and recently we had brought his furniture to the house from the storage and gotten rid of most of mine. He had been tired of paying for the storage and Penny was living with her boyfriend. So he decided that since it was nicer than what I had we would use it.

The first day we had it, he said that the kids weren't allowed to sit on it as they might wreck it. That was really funny, as it wasn't in very good shape. I didn't see how they could wreck it by sitting on it. I told him in that case to take it right back out of the house as my kids were allowed to sit on the furniture in my house. He didn't say anything about it after that.

I was very upset to find out that he had cheated on me. So I just decided to take my heart out of the equation. It actually made it easier for me as he couldn't hurt me if I didn't care about him. I would work on finding another source of income and getting my independence back and then he could leave. But, in the meantime I would let him believe that I had forgiven him after a period of making him sleep on the couch. As far as I was concerned he could sleep there forever.

A week or two later, Aunt Karen invited me to a lingerie home party. I wasn't much in the mood for lingerie as I wasn't planning on having any man in my life that I needed to impress with sexy undergarments and I hated home parties. So I declined her invitation. I told her to get me a catalogue and I would take a look at it. I thought I might find something useful just to help her out with her party sales. Instead of getting a catalogue she gave the sales agent my phone number and apparently told her that she thought I might have a party at my home. I was furious, but agreed to let the agent come over and talk to me. She was very nice on

46

the phone and it wasn't her fault that Karen had misinformed her.

When she came to show me the lingerie and explained how the party plan worked and how much fun it was doing the parties, I told her I would give it some thought. It actually did sound like a great way to make some extra money and I was looking for a way to do that and still be home with my kids. As well, it wasn't a fixed income like working for someone else. I could earn as much as I wanted depending on how hard I was willing to work. At that time in my life I was willing to work very hard if the money was there. The sooner I was earning a good income, the sooner I could get rid of Jeff. He was still kissing my ass and doing everything he could to get back into my good graces, so he was more than happy to look after the kids if I wanted to do the parties.

He also encouraged me to take advantage of the opportunity to make money, so I decided to give it a shot. My recruiter Colleen would do the presentations at my first few shows and train me at the same time. From those shows I would do the presentations at any other shows booked and I would be on my way. My first few parties that Colleen did were very successful and getting women to buy the lingerie and book shows was very easy. The product line was top quality and men would give their wives and girlfriends money to buy themselves something.

I started earning an average of $100 to $150 per show and holding 8-10 shows per month. I was earning 25% of my sales and they were good. I loved that I got paid to party for a living. I got out of the house for a couple of hours and had adult female time. The best payoff was the amazing people that I met and that touched my life in so many different ways. Sometimes things got to be more complicated and frustrating than they were worth, but I was determined to take it in stride and work my way up the ladder until I was earning a solid income.

One of the women from Jeff's work, the wife of one of his co-workers, held a party for me. Her name was Darla and she was a riot-loud, proud and deservedly so. She ended up holding several parties for me and the sales per show were usually about $1000. She loved the lingerie, was getting lots of it free and I was making great commissions. She had a friend who was a psychic and invited Jeff and I to a party at her salon.

Darla was a nail technician and manicurist with her own shop, where she did a fabulous job. I loved having my nails long, but when my relationships went south, so did my fingernails. If men would pay attention they wouldn't be so shocked when I up and left. If I was biting my nails, the relationship was in big trouble. It was just a matter of how much longer it would last.

I adored Darla and told her that of course we would go. It was $25 per person and we got to have a private reading. I had always enjoyed having my fortune told, although I didn't take it too seriously. It was fun to see if anything actually came true. The night of the party there were several people there and we sat around chatting as each person went in for their reading. Cindy, the psychic had not met any of us beforehand, but had gone directly into the other room where she would see us individually first.

I went in before Jeff and many of the things she told me were very interesting. I didn't tell Jeff that she said we would not be together too much longer and when we split I would be fine. I didn't really need a psychic to tell me that! She told me about each of my kids too. My oldest daughter Susan was my serious child, who had a very warm heart. Middle child Arthur was a bit of a troublemaker and would stretch my patience to the limit. Many years later, he did just that. Baby Jen was my free spirit. She said that if Susan and Jen were walking down the street and saw an injured bird, Susan would be the type of person that would bend down, pick up the bird and bring it home to take care of. Jen, on the other hand, would bend down and say, "Oh, poor bird", then go merrily on her way.

As my children grew up I realized that Cindy had pretty much been right about all of them. One thing I found most interesting was that she saw me driving a small blue car and that I needed that car to make my living. I drove a primer red van at the time, but she said that the blue car was not necessarily right then, but sometime in the near future. I took it all with a grain of salt at the time and was very entertained, but later in my life I would find it a bit spooky.

After the party, Jeff told me that Cindy saw two women in his life, one past and one present. The past one, she said was the pickle up his ass and the present one (me) was his rock and the one he could depend on. She also told him that he would not be with the present woman for very long if he weren't careful. Once she was gone, he would bounce around like a rubber ball for a long time before he settled down again. He thought it was all very amusing and believed we were settled for life, even though I kept telling him I had decided I would never marry him. Some people just don't get it.

It didn't take long before her predictions about the kids started coming true. Arthur and Jen were both giving me grief, getting into trouble together. One morning I was sleeping when Susan came running downstairs to tell me that the house was on fire. I jumped out of bed and ran up the stairs to find the main floor full of smoke. I didn't see any flames, but smoke was coming from the kitchen. I yelled to Jeff that I was taking the kids out of the house as he went to the kitchen to see where the fire was. Outside, I told Susan to stay with Arthur and Jen while I went back in to help Jeff.

In the kitchen Jeff and I still couldn't see any flames, but found a chair next to the stove! One of the burners was red hot and that's where the smoke was coming from. Jeff turned the burner off and I ran around opening doors and windows to clear out the smoke. When it had cleared enough to see, we discovered the lid of a juice jug almost melted away on the burner. From the looks of it, the whole plastic jug had melted and filled the pan at the bottom of the burner. It took hours to clear out the smoke and days to get rid of the smell.

It turned out that Arthur, who was only 4 at the time, was the one who had pulled the chair over to the stove and turned on the burner. I didn't know if the jug had already been on the burner or if he had put it there, but either way it could have been a lot worse. We had smoke detectors located just outside the kitchen in the hallway, but they had not gone off until the smoke had started to clear.

I was terrified that one day Arthur would burn the house down. I talked to Grandma about it and she said I should tie him into his bed at night. I couldn't imagine tying my child to a bed! Grandma said to get one of the harness's made for small children, put Arthur in it, then tie a piece of rope to either side of the bed. She said the rope should be loose enough to give him freedom to move around, but short enough so that he couldn't get off the bed. I didn't have another solution, so I decided to give it a try.

It seemed to work fine, but it wasn't long before he figured out how to undo the harness and get out of it. The only other thing I could think to do was to put a lock on the door of the bedroom he and Jen shared, so that he couldn't get out at night. I put a chain lock on the outside of the bedroom, so that he could still open the door a few inches, but not far enough to get out. I hoped that would solve the problem.

As if I didn't already have enough problems, Jeff wasn't helping matters any. He had started buying cocaine and bringing it home. The next thing I knew he was dealing it. The stuff he was getting was 80% pure and he was cutting it himself. It wasn't long before I started snorting it with him at night when the kids had gone to bed and a short time later, Jeff started doing it during the day as well.

He would lock himself in the basement and do it with a needle. There was no way I was sticking any needles in my arm and I was trying not to do it at all, but it was hard when it was always there. What he was keeping for personal use was more pure than what he was selling and he would leave lines set up on a mirror behind the bar in our bedroom. It was easy to do anytime I wanted and hard to resist. I found myself doing it far too much. I was still able to take care of the kids, but often wondered how.

CHAPTER SIX

1987

Drugs

One night, my friend Kevin and a mutual friend of ours, Larry Dean, came over to the house, along with his girlfriend Jodie. That's when things really started getting out of order. I had never known Kevin to be into drugs, rarely even smoking pot. Larry had apparently been into cocaine for a while though. Jodie had snorted it before, but never hit it with a needle and Larry convinced her that it was a better high when done that way. I saw Kevin doing a hit and couldn't even watch. I was so disappointed to see him walking down that road, even though I was doing it myself. I wasn't very happy about my drug use and even more upset by Kevin's. He was too sweet to get messed up on drugs. First, Larry did a hit then mixed one up for Jodie. I hated needles from the doctor and turned away whenever anyone did a hit. I was so turned off by it that I didn't even want to do any at all or be around it, so I went upstairs to get away from them.

A few minutes later, Jeff called for me to hurry downstairs, that something was wrong with Jodie. I hated hearing those words. It was always something really bad. I followed him downstairs and found Jodie on the floor having convulsions. She was foaming at the mouth, her lips were turning blue and I had no idea what to do. Larry had obviously mixed the hit too strong for her and she was overdosing. I had never had any experience with an overdose and panicked. I didn't know if I should call 911, knowing that the police would come and I could lose my children. I just wanted for it not to be happening. None of my choices seemed likely to result in my children being allowed to remain with me.

Larry, oblivious to the whole situation, was busy mixing himself a hit behind the bar and I was flabbergasted that he could even think about it right then. I wanted him to take her away from my house and get her medical attention. I couldn't let her die there in the basement. Jeff and Kevin were doing what they could to revive her and just when I thought I was going to have to call 911, she started to come around.

Gradually she came back to consciousness and we could tell that she would be all right. I told Larry to get her out of my place and help her straighten out. When the others left I turned to Jeff and told him to get all the cocaine and paraphernalia out of the house! I never wanted to see it there again. As far as I know he never did bring any in the house again.

I think he must have been doing it somewhere else though, or hiding it. One night it seemed to me like he was obviously on something. We hadn't seen or heard anything from Kevin for a couple of months since the Jodie incident. His name hadn't even come up in conversation since then. I didn't understand why Kevin would even be on Jeff's mind, but this particular night, he managed to work himself into quite a state over him. I was fast asleep when he came home and woke me up yelling and screaming something about Kevin. I couldn't tell what he was saying, but the impression I got was that he was jealous or something.

When he got to the bed, he started punching me all over. I was frozen by shock for a couple of minutes before I reached out from under the blanket with one leg and kicked him square in the face. He stopped immediately and when he put his hand to his nose there was blood running from it. "You broke my nose", he yelled.

"Yes, I did and if you ever raise your hands to me again I will kill you!" I shouted right back at him.

He turned and walked away slowly, but I was right

behind him yelling, "You can start packing your shit and get out of here!"

I was fuming and beginning to feel the effects of his fists on my ribs and legs. I didn't want any more confrontation that night, so I decided the best thing for me to do was to go back to bed until he straightened out. I would deal with him then.

Apparently, Jeff had other ideas and just as I was drifting back to sleep I heard the door open and Jeff coming down the stairs. He was mumbling something that I couldn't understand, so I sat up to see what his problem was. To my horror I saw that his wrists were bleeding and he was crying that if he couldn't be with me he didn't want to be anywhere. "Oh great", I thought to myself, "now he's really lost it."

I jumped up, put on my robe and tried to find something to wrap around his wrists. He didn't want any help from me and as soon as he figured out what I was attempting to do he took off upstairs. I followed as he went into the kitchen drawer and took out a steak knife. I had no idea what he planned to do with it and backed down the stairs far enough to close the door behind me, holding on to it. I knew that if he wanted to get through the door I probably wouldn't be able to stop him anyway, as he was stronger than I was.

I was concerned that he may go upstairs where the kids were sleeping, so I was listening for his footsteps to keep track of him. I didn't hear a sound for a minute or two and thought I had better take a look and see where he was. I opened the door a couple of inches and just as I did I heard the front door open and close. When I looked all the way out, I saw that the front door was open. I ran to the door and looked outside, but couldn't see any sign of him. I had never seen him like that before and he was so unpredictable that I knew I needed help, so I called 911.

The fact that this crazy man was out on the streets

with a knife in his hand gave reason for the police to arrive rather quickly and begin an immediate search of the area. I described to two of the officers what had happened. The added information that he was also high on cocaine and suicidal gave them cause for great concern. I went back inside to put some clothes on, as I was still in my robe with all the cops wandering around. When I went into the basement and shut the door, Jeff popped up from behind the bed. He must have snuck in the back door while I was busy talking to the police. He was whispering to me to not tell them that he was there and I found that hilarious, as I was the one who had called them there and wanted him out. I turned right back up the stairs and alerted the closest officer that Jeff was in the basement, but I didn't know if he was still armed. When Jeff realized that they had him he raised his hands to show that he was unarmed and came up the stairs.

He started swearing and calling me names. I walked away and went into the other room to leave him for the cops to handle. One of them went with me and I could hear the others trying to calm Jeff down, so he could talk to them and tell his version of the story. The officer who remained with me explained that they could take him out of the house for now, but that he would be allowed to return in the morning as he lived there. I would have to go through the courts to have him removed. He wasn't even on the lease, but that didn't matter as long as it was his known residence.

They didn't really manage to get Jeff calmed down. He kept following me around the room and calling me names, saying that he hated me. I told him to just stop talking to me and leave me alone if he hated me so much. The cops were having a hard time getting through to him and asked me if I felt it was safe to leave him with me. I told them that under no circumstances did I see that as an option. One of us was sure to wind up dead.

Under those conditions, they decided they could force him to go to the hospital and charge him with possession of a deadly weapon. I told them to just do whatever they had to in order to remove him. I didn't want to press assault charges, but I wanted him away from me for the time being.

The next day when I woke up I could hardly move. My whole body felt like it had been hit by a Mack truck and I found it very difficult to hide that fact from the children. I told them that I wasn't feeling well and they accepted that.

However, the following day, I had a meeting to go to with Colleen and as soon as she saw me she asked what was wrong. I couldn't help gasping when I moved in certain ways. My ribs and legs were bruised and Colleen also noticed that I had a bruise on my temple. She questioned me about it, asking point blank if Jeff had done it. We weren't as close then as we would later become, so I told her that Jeff hadn't done anything and I was fine. She didn't press any further, but we both knew that she knew what had happened. We just weren't comfortable enough with each other to talk about it.

Jeff came home the following day with his wrists bandaged and nobody said anything about it, even though I knew that the kids had to have heard most of what had gone on. When they went to bed that night I tried to reassure them that they didn't have to worry about anything and everything would be fine. As far as they were concerned Jeff was their dad, with the exception of Susan. Arthur and Jen had been calling him Dad in some form or another since they started talking.

Jeff of course, was back to being sweet and apologetic. He didn't know what had come over him, but he was afraid that I was going to leave him and he couldn't live without me and blah-blah-blah. He had reason to be worried.

He would be gone the first chance I had, but he was making me feel guilty about it. I was worried that if I left him he would kill himself and I would have to live with that on my conscience for the rest of my life. He sure knew how to get around me and before long the charges were dropped. Things were gradually getting back to the way they had been. He slept on the couch again for a while and kissed my ass all over the place until he started feeling secure again.

CHAPTER SEVEN

1987

The Step Children

Just when I thought things were finally settling down, chaos started again. Much to our surprise, Jeff's delight and my chagrin, Penny called and told him that she had decided it would be best for their kids to live with us after all. They were living in a low-income apartment complex that had a store on the property for the convenience of the tenants. Their apartment had previously been the home of a little girl who disappeared a year or so earlier. The girl had been kidnapped and it was big news all over the country when it happened, but she hadn't been found.

One day, Jeff's children had gone down to the store in their apartment complex and it was being robbed by a young man holding a knife to the proprietor's throat. The kids were terrified and that was the turning point for Penny. She thought that perhaps the children would be safer in our neighborhood. We arranged to pick them up the next day and agreed that when Penny got herself together they could go back to live with her. She was moving in with her boyfriend Joe, until she could arrange suitable housing for herself and the children.

With the coming of an additional three children to our household, Jeff and I had to do some rearranging of the bedrooms. My kids each had their own room, but the prospect of having two sisters and a brother move in with them seemed like an adventure, so they were happy to share their space.

Jeff's daughter Teresa was 13, and deserved to have some privacy, so I decided to let her have her own room. I even painted it for her and made curtains to match. Jeff and I gave her a portable stereo and helped her decorate the room to her liking. Jeff's younger daughter Jane shared a room with Susan. We gave them the bedroom with the waterbed I had given Susan when Jeff and I brought his things out of storage. That left Jeff's son Brian to share with Arthur and they got the bunk beds in the other bedroom, along with Jen's crib.

Teresa was interested in making some extra money and would do some babysitting for us. I told her that if I found her to be reliable I would recommend her to other people and try to help her earn some extra cash. She had done a lot of babysitting while living with her mother and I heard she was good at it. Before long I was ready to give her a reference. My brother Bruce's ex-wife Deirdre and my niece Natasha lived nearby, so I let Deirdre know that Teresa was available if she needed her. Soon she began having Teresa over to babysit Natasha.

The kids were all getting along great. Although we had a few squabbles now and then, it seemed as if they were really siblings and we were one big happy family. Ironically, just as I was starting to enjoy the idea of being one big happy family, we started having problems with Teresa. She was coming in past curfew, playing her stereo too loud and talking back to both of us. I understood that making an adjustment to her new life was hard, as it was for everyone, but at the same time we had to have some semblance of order. Deirdre seemed happy with the job she was doing babysitting. She and Natasha got along well and Deirdre was thrilled to have someone she felt safe leaving Natasha with.

At least until one day Deirdre called me to say that while babysitting, Teresa had apparently stolen a $200 gold chain belonging to Deirdre's roommate. It had been left on her roommate's dresser when they went out and was gone when they got home. I was very disappointed and felt like Teresa had betrayed my trust. I told Deirdre that she should call the police and file charges against Teresa, so that she would hopefully learn an important lesson while she was still a minor.

When the police came to the house to arrest Teresa she asked me to go to the station with her instead of Jeff. I was very angry with her for betraying my trust, but at the same time I knew how scared she was and didn't want her to have to go alone. Jeff was just angry and didn't seem concerned about her feelings at all, so I went with her.

I was rather touched that she asked me and stood by her while she was charged, fingerprinted and finally released. Of course we had to punish her at home as well and I told her that she was grounded, not allowed out except to go to school. When she asked how long she was grounded for, I told her that I thought until she went to court would be appropriate. Her court date was six weeks away, so she was not happy about that, but I felt that what she had done was serious enough to warrant a long period of punishment. She still had her stereo in her room and was free to do as she had done at home before, but not allowed to hang out with her friends.

She was very good about it for the first couple of weeks and didn't give us any problems. Then Jeff called her for dinner one day and she didn't come downstairs. After waiting a few minutes he went up to get her and found her room empty. Her window, only a few feet off the ground, was open, so we assumed she had gone out the window. Jeff was furious and immediately went out to look for her. He came back with her an hour or so later and she went straight to her room without a word. Jeff told me that he had found her at the mall with her friends. He had grabbed her by her jacket and dragged her out to the car. She had fought him all the way and by the time he got her into the car a police car had pulled up. Someone in the mall had thought that she was being abducted and called them.

When Jeff calmed down enough to explain the situation to the police they let him leave with her. As he explained it to me he got even angrier. As soon as he had finished telling me the story, he went up to her room and came back down with her stereo. He told me that as of right then she was grounded to her room except for meals and chores and would not be getting the stereo back any time soon. I thought he was being a little harsh, but chose not to interfere. I did suggest that perhaps it was time to try and get her some counseling to help her deal with whatever it was that was upsetting her. He agreed that I could make the arrangements and I called our doctor the following day.

Fortunately, the counselor just happened to have a cancellation for a couple of days later, so we set up an appointment quickly. I took her alone to her assessment, to see if she actually needed the counseling. At the end of it, the therapist told me he would like to see the whole family the next time. I wasn't thrilled about that, but he explained that it would help Teresa if he knew more about the environment and personalities she was dealing with. I told him that my two youngest children were only three and four years old. He said he could still tell a lot about them by watching how they played and interacted with the rest of us - and by how we interacted with them.

The following week the entire family went for a session. The doctor spoke to each of us and drew a family tree. He asked a lot of questions and Teresa sat in her chair silently throughout the session. At the end of it he said that if we had no objections he would like to videotape our sessions for research purposes or some stupid thing like that. I told him none of us would be attending further sessions. We were not his guinea pigs! Teresa had issues that she was having a hard time dealing with and I suspected they had more to do with her mother than with us. That was what we had gone to him for. He said he would still like to see the entire family for future sessions, so I told him I would think about it. I was not willing to take the other children out of school for half a day every week when we weren't having any real problems with them.

Jeff was just fed up with having to deal with any of it and he was angry most of the time. I told Teresa that if she went out her window again her bags would be packed when she got back. I made it clear to her that she could go back to her mother or the CAS. I didn't care which. Jeff had left me pretty much in charge of six kids and I wasn't putting up with any more of her crap. If she didn't like the rules she didn't have to live with us. I had done everything I could to welcome her and her siblings into our home and she was making it hard for everyone.

Sure enough a couple of days later, she went out her window again. I told Jeff to call CAS, while I packed her clothes and by the time she came back they were waiting by the front door. We called CAS when she returned and the worker was there within a short time. It really did hurt my heart to send her back to a foster home, but she was old enough to make certain decisions and she knew the consequences. We had a house full of children and after all I had done to help her, I was not about to put up with her disrespecting me that way.

Once Teresa left, we found it much easier to deal with the rest of the children. Jane was a quiet little red head, with a face full of freckles. She was good for the most part, but had a bit of a bad attitude. We figured that was because she was angry with her mother for not being able to take care of her, as she was often very vocal on the subject. I thought once she got used to living with us she would calm down and sure enough, she did. After a very short time she and Susan bonded and behaved like real sisters. Sometimes they got along and sometimes they didn't. To me that was normal. I understood that it was difficult for all of the children to integrate into a new family, so a little extra patience would go a long way.

Brian was a cutie, with the same red hair and freckles that Jane had. He was also very angry with Penny and was doing some acting out. We decided not to continue the counseling after Teresa left and after a little while everyone settled into a routine.

One day, we got a call from school. It was about Brian and the teacher wanted us to meet with her to discuss it. Jeff went to the school to see what was going on and said that apparently Brian had pushed a girl down on the ground. The teacher found him sitting on top of her with his hands around her throat. The story was that Brian had told the little girl that he was going to put her in a cage and rape her. Her parents were understandably very upset - as we were. He was only six years old at the time and I wasn't sure he really understood what he had said. I asked him if he knew what rape meant and he said that it meant he was going to tie her up. I explained to him what it actually meant in as simple terms as I could and he was very upset. I told him that he needed to apologize to her and that he should never use words unless he knew what they meant. Once he apologized to the girl and her parents it was the end of that situation.

Then I became concerned with my son, Arthur. I thought he was jealous of Brian or something as I caught him in the living room one day, approaching Brian from behind with a steak knife. Brian was absorbed in a TV show and Arthur had the knife raised over his head as if he were going to stab him in the back. I screamed at Arthur, which also caught Brian's attention, as I grabbed the knife from Arthur's hand. He was too young to be able to grasp the concept of death, so I didn't think he had actually been trying to kill Brian, or even seriously hurt him, but I became very watchful of his behavior after that. I tried to explain to him what would have happened if he had stabbed Brian, but I wasn't really sure how much he could understand. He was only four. All I knew was that I couldn't handle all the bullshit alone and Jeff seemed to have lost interest in taking care of his own kids, never mind helping with mine.

Somehow, I still managed to keep up with my lingerie business. It was going very well and I was looking forward to attending a convention in the summer. Things were looking up. Life was beginning to be less of a struggle than it had been before.

CHAPTER EIGHT

1987

Uncle Doug's Wedding

It was during the summer that my Uncle Doug, who was in his mid thirties, decided to end his bachelor days and finally take the plunge by marrying his girlfriend Fiona. I was so happy for him, since he had always been my favorite Uncle.

I had some wonderful childhood memories of Uncle Doug. When I was 8, he was the one who decided it was time for me to learn how to ride a bike. He took me across the street to the high school parking lot and gave me lessons. It took quite some time to get it right, but he was patient. After awhile I was able to ride a little ways by myself and then it just took some practice until I was actually pretty good at it. I was always grateful to him for taking the time to teach me.

Uncle Doug was also the one that inspired me to learn to water-ski. He was an amazing skier and could ski slalom. He started off from the beach instead of in the water and would go back and forth over the wake from the boat, making a big spray behind him. Grandma told me that one time he tried to start off from the wooden raft and when he took off, the seat of his bathing suit stayed on the raft. She laughed her head off when she told the story and once you got her laughing it was contagious. When she and Aunt Karen started laughing at something together, it was hard to get them to stop.

It took me about four consecutive summers, skiing every weekend, to finally conquer slalom. Perhaps 'conquer' is the wrong word to use, (let's just say I could go once around without falling). Funny enough, as life would have it, when I finally got the hang of it that turned out to be the last time that I ever water-skied.

Uncle Doug's wedding ceremony and reception were held at Pioneer Village. The guests were greeted at the entrance by a horse and buggy and driven through the village to the tiny church. The church was lit up with candles and the whole ceremony was very old fashioned, right down to the bride and groom's attire. Fiona wore an Edwardian style gown with a high lace neckline and large front lace yoke. The sleeves were full at the upper arm and tightly tapered from elbow to wrist, ending in a point over her hands. The bodice was fitted through the waistline and the skirt portion had a very slight flair elegantly gathered in the back. It didn't have a long train as the modern dresses do, but a large lace bow on the back of the waistline. Doug wore a cutaway coat and ascot in black with striped pants. His shirt had a stand up collar, known as a winged-collar shirt and they both looked very elegant.

After the ceremony we all walked down the road to a restaurant, while the bride and groom had pictures taken. After the pictures Uncle Doug and my new Aunt Fiona were driven by horse and buggy to meet the rest of us. Mom, Jeff and I tried to find seats at the table farthest from my grandparents so we could drink wine and smoke if we wanted to. With Grandpa being a minister and all we couldn't do that within sight of them. Unfortunately, we ended up seated at the very same table, just at the other end. I decided that I didn't care what they thought. I was just going to be myself and enjoy the party. If they didn't like it, it was too bad.

After dinner there was music and dancing. At one point, I was standing up watching people dance when Uncle Hector came over to ask me to dance. I just glared at him, then turned and walked away. I couldn't believe the nerve of him, like he was oblivious to the fact that I couldn't stand being in the same room as him, never mind actually paying any attention to him. Dance with him? If he and I were the last two people on earth, there still was no chance that would ever happen.

I needed to go outside and get some fresh air, just to get away from him. When I went to get Jeff, Mom said that she would join us; apparently they had already been talking about it. When we got outside we walked a little ways from the restaurant and Jeff lit a joint. Mom knew that I smoked weed and I had even smoked it with her a couple of times, but I was surprised nonetheless. The three of us smoked it and it was funny getting high with Mom; she had a great time. I thought it was great to have a mom that was so cool and was more like a sister. She certainly understood and shared my hatred of Uncle Hector.

I was about nine years old when Aunt Lydia started dating Hector. They made a funny looking couple because he was over six feet tall and she was just four feet. I always loved spending time with Aunt Lydia and we were very close. Maybe because she was really short she didn't seem so much like a grown up as the other adults in the house did. She was also my Sunday school teacher for a couple of years and would always give me Bible verses to memorize each week. I always did extra verses because I had a good memory and it made her so proud to hear me recite them. I really loved Aunt Lydia, so I was very happy for her when she found a man that was interested in her, but there was something about him that was kind of creepy.

****

Frog in My Pocket

It was the summer of 1968. I was turning 10 and Aunt Karen was 12 at the time. Aunt Lydia invited both Karen and I to go camping at Georgian Bay with her and Hector, who was now her fiancé. Hector would take Karen and I for long

67

walks in the woods. Aunt Lydia had to stay behind at the trailer due to the condition the Polio had left her in. She wasn't able to walk too far.

Hector always wore big, baggy pants with deep pockets and he would get Karen & I to take turns playing a game he called 'frog in my pocket'. He would tell us to put our hands way down deep in his pocket and feel around until we found 'the frog'. Being young girls we weren't scared of frogs and had even caught some with my brothers, so it sounded like a fun game to me, but it really wasn't. It made me feel very uncomfortable and the only thing I ever felt in there wasn't anything like a frog ...

****

In 1971 I was thirteen and Aunt Mavis gave birth to my cousin Julie. Aunt Mavis was Mom's older sister and she was a little on the serious side, but still fun to be around. Her husband, Uncle Lewis was an amateur comedian who made the whole family laugh with all his silliness. I loved going to their house to play in the backyard or to play pool in the basement. My brothers and I were very close to their three boys Paul, Ross and Terry, as we were all close in age, with me being the oldest.

Julie was a beautiful blonde-haired, blue-eyed angel. Up until then, I had been the only granddaughter for thirteen years and suddenly I had to share the spotlight with Julie, but I loved her so much that I was happy to. I really missed them all when they moved to Europe a couple of years later, knowing that Julie and I wouldn't be able to bond as her brothers and I had. Uncle Lewis was going there to work, so we wouldn't get to see them much, but could keep in touch through letters and photos.

Around the same time, I had another cousin when Aunt Lydia gave birth to Marvin. I loved babysitting him, which I often did. He was such a good baby that I adored him (still do) and learned to take good care of him.

The summer after Marvin was born we all went up to the cottage. Aunt Lydia had been having back problems and couldn't lift him, so she came to the family to help take care of him. That same summer, my Aunt Mavis and Uncle Lewis were there visiting with their family. There were two cottages on the property and my grandparents would usually rent one of them to friends or family. Aunt Mavis was also having back problems, so Aunt Karen and I were designated baby-sitters for Marvin and Julie. I didn't mind most of the time, but I was only fourteen, so there were times that I wanted to go off with my friends. Julie would cry and run after me and she was so sweet that I couldn't say no to her, so I ended up taking her with me or staying home.

When it was time for Lydia to go home it was decided that I would go with her to help look after Marvin as the doctor had ordered her not to lift him and he wasn't able to walk yet. It was only supposed to be for two weeks, so I was happy to help her out. They lived in a two-bedroom apartment, both of which were being used and I had to sleep on the couch in the living room.

Sometimes I would wake up at night and feel someone lifting up my nightgown. It was Hector and he was touching me under my gown. It made me very uncomfortable, but I was afraid to open my eyes and let him know that I was awake. He would be breathing really hard and his hands were sweaty and shaking. I would just stay very still and pray that he would go away. He usually did after a few minutes, but I wouldn't be able to go back to sleep for fear that he would come back and I would be too deeply asleep to wake up. God only knew what liberties he would take then.

One night he came home really late and I woke up when he bumped into the coffee table beside me. I pretended to be asleep and hoped that he would just go right to his room. Instead he came over to the couch and tried to uncover me, but I had learned to wrap the blanket tightly around me for protection. I tensed up so that he couldn't pull the blanket off. That didn't stop him and the next thing I knew he was lifting the blanket from the bottom, uncovering my legs and then he lifted up my nightie. I didn't feel him touching me for a moment, but I could feel him moving around close to me. I stayed very still and started praying really hard that he would go away.

I could smell his breath. It reeked of alcohol as I felt him trying to lie on top of me. I felt something funny touch my bottom. He started feeling around with his hand and tried to push my legs apart. I could feel something hard between my legs and it suddenly occurred to me what he was trying to do. I was a virgin, but I knew what intercourse was, that was how moms and dads made babies. I panicked and rolled over as fast as I could (he was a lot bigger than I was, but God must have given me the strength). He fell off onto the floor and I jumped up and started screaming at him that if he wanted to have sex he should go into the bedroom with his wife!

I was horrified and couldn't go back to sleep for the rest of the night. I just lay under my blanket shaking, crying and praying that he wouldn't come back. First thing in the morning I called my friend Franci and told her what had happened. She told her Dad and they told me to pack my bags, they were coming to get me right away. My parents had gone away for the weekend, so Franci let me stay at her house until they came home. I didn't tell Mom what had happened. I just told her that I didn't want to stay there anymore. She didn't like Hector so she wasn't surprised that I didn't either and didn't question me further.

The next time I ran into Hector at a family gathering he waited until he could get me alone and apologized for his behavior. He said that he had been drunk and that what he had done had been "very childish". I told him that it sure was and turned my back on him. At that time I had no idea the repercussions of what he had done. I was upset because he was married, and married to my aunt at that. He should only be making babies with his wife, not somebody else.

I never told anybody about what happened, except my friend Franci at the time, because I thought I had done something wrong, like making him think that I liked him or something. I had no doubt that I would be believed if I told and thought that if Aunt Lydia found out that he was fooling around on her she would leave him. Then how would she be able to take care of Marvin all alone? After all, there hadn't really been any damage done and if nobody found out everything would be okay. Lydia and Marvin would be taken care of and Hector had apologized. I just decided that I would never sleep at their house again and that would be the end of my problem.

CHAPTER NINE

1989

Family Secrets

Early in my career as a lingerie agent, Aunt Lydia had become involved in my business as a hostess, holding several parties in her home. She had also revealed to me that her family life was not what it appeared on the outside. Her husband Hector was abusive to the family and ruled with an iron fist. She inferred that on several occasions he was not above using corporal punishment on her or the children. That didn't surprise me at all since he had always seemed the type of person that was violent and of course, I knew what atrocities he was capable of.

She was not happy with him and had turned to someone else for comfort. In short, she was having an affair and chose to confide it to me. She told me that she was afraid to leave Hector as she thought that he would easily take custody of the children because of her physical disability. I had always told her that I would not let that happen and that I guaranteed she would never lose custody of the children to him. I had a secret that would ensure it and with any luck, keep him away from her children forever.

Shortly after I found out about Aunt Lydia's affair, Aunt Karen called. I hadn't spoken with her for quite some time. She called to see how the family was and whether or not I still had my sanity with all the children in the house. We exchanged niceties about our own families and then the conversation turned to a local news report. Over the previous couple of days the news media had been reporting the disappearance of a young girl who they thought had met with foul play. With Karen and I both being mothers, we were very sympathetic towards the girl's mother. It must be awful for her not to know what had happened to her child.

In recent years there had been many reports of other children missing and being sexually abused, beaten and in most cases killed by their captors. We both hoped that would not be the case this time. It turned out that the girl's body was found a few days later and she had been sexually abused and murdered.

In the course of our conversation, Karen suddenly, but rather nonchalantly said, "I was molested when I was young". My heart skipped a beat as I quickly asked, "By someone in the family?"

"Yes, but I can't say who".

"By Hector?" I asked.

"How did you know?"

I told her that Hector had also molested me when I was about thirteen or fourteen. Karen said she had been about the same age or younger and that it had happened several times over a period of five or six years. "Don't you remember when Lydia and Hector used to take us on those camping trips and he would take us for a walk and make us play, "*Frog in my pocket*?" Karen asked.

I told her that I did, but hadn't thought much of that at the time, other than it made me very uncomfortable. As she reminded me, it occurred to me what 'the frog' we had been looking for was. She also told me that there had been other times when she was sleeping that he had 'messed with her', but wouldn't say exactly how. I wasn't really surprised that it had happened to her too, as we were only two years apart, but what did shock me was that Karen went on to say that Hector had also attempted to fondle my cousin Julie's breasts in recent years. Julie would be about thirteen now. That seemed to be the age that he liked them – about 9 or 10 to early teens. I became very concerned about the fact that Hector had a daughter Lynn, who was almost ten.

73

What horrified me the most about all of this was that if only I had been courageous enough to come forward at the time he molested me, I could have saved his daughter from the same fate. I was overwhelmed with guilt and anger and told Karen that we had to do something about it. I had heard of many cases of child molestation where adults had come forward later and were able to press charges against their abusers. I decided that was what we had to do. The police and our family had to know what that animal had been up to and stop him before he could hurt any more children.

Up until the time that Karen had revealed her secret to me, I had been under the assumption that what Hector had done to me had been only happening to me. It never occurred to me that he had been abusing other children as well. I didn't know if I thought I was 'special' in some way or what, but I still hadn't any idea the implications of his actions on my life. That realization would come several years later.

That first night when Hector had tried to rape me, I had told Franci's father. He was the only adult I had told and he hadn't told anyone else as far as I knew. Several years later, I told my brother Bruce and while he had been outraged about it at the time, he hadn't said anything more about it. Whenever the subject of sexual abuse came up he would end the conversation and refuse to discuss it.

The day that Aunt Lydia met with me and told me about her affair, she had also said that she was ready to ask Hector for a divorce. She knew that I had something on him that would help her retain custody of her children and she needed to know what that was before she could proceed with confidence. I told her to think it over because if I told her what I knew about Hector it would change her life forever and there would be no turning back. Of course, at the time I had no idea that he had molested anyone else. She told me that she was sure of her decision and wanted to know my secret. I told her about the night that he had attempted to rape me in their apartment, still thinking that the worst of it had been the fact that he was married to my aunt.

She was distraught, but it didn't seem to me that her reaction was appropriate to the information I had given her. It was as if she already knew. She thanked me for giving her the ammunition she would need to file for divorce and keep her children. She asked me not to say anything about it to anyone else just yet, and that when the time was right she would use what I had told her against him. Until then, she would appreciate my continued silence. I agreed that I would leave it up to her to decide when I should come forward and to whom.

Of course I hadn't heard back from Lydia on the subject and that had been several months before. As far I knew she also hadn't filed for divorce. Once I knew that other children had been involved it was beginning to dawn on me that it was a much more serious issue than I had thought and the time to speak up had come. I told Karen that I was going to the police to file charges and she agreed that she would as well. She said that she couldn't go to them on her own, but that if they called her she would talk to them and tell them what had happened to her.

I went to the police and told them my story and they had me repeat it for them on videotape. That way they would have the video for court when his case got that far and it might not be necessary for me to endure the trauma of having to sit in a courtroom with Hector and talk about it. They told me that Karen and Julie would have to come forward and tell their stories as well, to corroborate mine. I assured them that Karen would talk to them and expressed my concern for Hector's youngest child, Lynn. They recommended that I contact the Children's Aid Society and file a report with them, giving them the name of the detective who would be handling my case.

I called CAS and filed a report and also called Mom to tell her what was going on. She was devastated and couldn't bring herself to have a conversation with me about it. She explained to me several months later that she couldn't deal with what had happened to me because then she would have to deal with the abuse that she had experienced as a child. I felt her pain and asked her to explain to me what had happened to her. "Let's just say that I was shown things that a young child should not be shown", she told me. I asked her who had abused her and she said that it had been someone at our church. I came out with the name James Whitman right away and wasn't surprised when she told me I was right. She was shocked and wanted to know how I had known.

Truth be told, I didn't know how I knew, I just did. Perhaps it was better that I didn't know how I had come up with his name so quickly. I decided to let my mother be and not discuss the situation with her unless I had to. I could only imagine how painful it was for her to know that her daughter had been sexually molested and I didn't want her to hurt because of it. I also assured her that I didn't blame her in any way. How could she have known?

I was grateful then that Mom had Dad to lean on. When I was thirteen, Mom and Arthur finally got married. He was fun most of the time, and very intelligent. When they first started dating he worked as an auto mechanic. Later, he began teaching it at a high school. After eight years of dating Mom, he had been offered a job in Nigeria as Dean of a school and he was considering going. They talked to my brothers and I about it and said that if he decided to take us with him, we would have to ride camels to school. I didn't know if they were kidding or not, but it sounded kind of cool to me.

Mom told me afterwards that if he decided to go without us it would be for two years and she wasn't going to wait around for him to get back unless he wanted to marry her. Thankfully, he asked her to marry him and we all stayed at home. From the day they got married he wouldn't answer to Arthur anymore, just to Dad. Many years later, when I gave birth to my son, I decided to name him Arthur, after my dad.

A few days after speaking with the police, the CAS worker that I had filed a report with contacted me. She wanted to let me know that she had gone to see Hector and Lydia and told them of my allegations. Hector admitted to CAS that he molested Karen and I as children, but assured them that it had been a one-time thing and that it never happened again. He said he had not abused any other children and certainly not his own daughter. The worker had spoken to Lynn and concluded that her father was not molesting her, so they allowed Lynn to remain in the home.

I knew in my heart that Hector was full of crap and couldn't believe that the worker had left Lynn there. She was a young child and she wasn't likely to admit easily that he had touched her. She still had to live with him and didn't know what would happen if she talked about it. He could deny it all he wanted, but in my heart I knew better.

Later, I called my Aunt Mavis and told her what Karen had told me about Julie. She said that she would speak to Julie about it and see what she had to say. I heard back that Julie had stopped Hector from fondling her, that it was "no big deal", and that she would just as soon forget about it. Apparently, so would Mavis and her husband, Lewis. I was appalled that my family just wanted to sweep the whole situation under the rug and forget about it like it never happened.

I was concerned about my grandparents finding out and had no intention of telling them. They were old and had a lot of health problems by then, along with Grandpa being a minister and all. I was pretty sure the rest of the family felt the same way. I did think however, that the rest of us could all work together to ensure the safety of the younger children in the family.

It was beyond my comprehension that the older generation just wanted to pretend that it didn't happen. It was as if what Hector had done wasn't really okay, but it wasn't really that bad either. I had always known my family to be very close and loving, but it didn't seem like they loved me enough to defend me against someone who had done unspeakable things to me. I just didn't understand how they could be so casual about such a serious issue, especially when he could be doing the same thing to his own daughter and many other children. I shuddered to think of all the children he had access to as a Cub Scout leader. Weren't adults supposed to protect innocent children?

Aunt Karen also decided that it would be best to just leave the past in the past and told the police that she didn't want to file charges. I couldn't believe that she of all people would refuse to back me up. My mother was furious with her. They didn't have a close relationship as it was, but Mom wanted as little as possible to do with her or Aunt Lydia from then on. She only spoke to them when she had to at family gatherings to keep my grandparents happy. She swore that once both of my grandparents were gone she wouldn't speak to either of them again.

So there I was, alone in my fight for justice. Without corroborating witnesses I didn't have a leg to stand on. Hector won again and I had no choice but to drop it. I had nobody to support me. The only other victims that I knew about were both too young and scared to talk about it, or too scared to make waves in the family. I started feeling different about my close, loving family then.

They didn't seem to understand that my concern was not for me, but for the other children that were unprotected from someone who I knew for a fact was a pedophile. I was an adult now and he couldn't hurt me anymore, but he had been a Cub Scout Leader for many years, which put him into contact with many young children. He also had a daughter that I was sure was already being molested.

I was astounded by the attitude of my family. Just leave it in the past!? My feeling was that they thought our family was too good to bring shame on us by speaking up about a pedophile in our midst. It wasn't like he was blood, but I figured anyone in our family marrying someone like that would be shame enough. I felt like screaming, "He is NOT a member of our family. He just married into it and we certainly don't owe any loyalty to him! What about blood?"

Even if he had been blood, that shouldn't have made a difference. What he did was just plain wrong and those who knew should not be protecting him. They should be protecting his innocent victims. I was left very angry and frustrated and thinking that perhaps I was making too much of it. Everyone else seemed to think it wasn't such a big deal and the other victims and I were fine. So why make trouble? I had no choice at the time, but to try to forget about it and get on with my life.

CHAPTER TEN

1989

A New Home

Believe it or not, I did have other things to worry about, like finding a new place to live. Our landlord called and said that they had decided to move back into the house as his company was transferring him back to Canada from the U.S. We had two months to find a new place and move out. That was really okay with me as I was finding it getting crowded where we were and hoped we could find something bigger. We wanted to try and stay in the same area if we could as the kids liked it and it was convenient for schools and shopping.

Jeff told me to go ahead and look for a place and he would just trust my judgment. He really didn't care where we lived, as long as it was okay for me. What he really meant was that it was my job to take care of the house and the kids, so as long as the place was okay with me, he'd just as soon not bother with doing the work of finding one. Along with everything else, that would be left up to me.

Within a couple of weeks I found a townhouse in a nearby neighborhood that we could afford. Even though it didn't give us more space, I thought it would be suitable for a while. The backyard was very small, but I had found that we hadn't been using the yard that much anyway. We would be able to manage with the smaller one.

There were three bedrooms upstairs, so the two older girls could continue to share a room. The boys would share one and Jen would have her own room. She had a tendency to get into other peoples' things, so it would be better to have her in a different room. The basement was finished, so Jeff and I would use that as our bedroom and there was enough room to set up an office area for my business. There was also a good size storage room with shelving on all the walls, so it would be great for my craft and other business supplies. The only real down side was that there was no closet, but we figured we could put up some kind of a bar for hanging our clothes and I had garment racks for my lingerie samples. That way, we would also have a divider between the bedroom and office areas.

Everyone was thrilled that we were moving, especially Jeff's kids. This would be a place that we all moved into together and they would feel like it was just as much their home as the rest of the family. I just couldn't wait to get through all the work of packing, moving and unpacking.

We got the move over with and everyone got settled into our new home in no time. Our old neighborhood had been predominantly white residents, but the new one was not. I was glad that the kids had the opportunity to socialize with people of other ethnicities, unlike when I was young. I didn't want them to grow up with the same prejudices that my family had as I felt they would be much happier if they got along with all cultures.

I couldn't understand the reasons for my family's attitudes and thought the whole racist thing was stupid. Our religion taught that we were all God's children, yet they were against interracial relationships. We had a black family in the next house and the kids all got to be very good friends. They also got to be friends with two brothers who lived across the street that were black. Susan quickly became best friends with another girl down the street.

Once we were settled the kids started asking for a pet, specifically a dog. I wasn't crazy about the idea even though I loved dogs, but I knew that I would be the one left with the responsibility of feeding and cleaning up after it. I told them we would have to wait a while and see how responsible they were with doing their chores and cleaning up after themselves first.

Business was booming and I was looking forward to the release of our new Holiday Collection, which would be presented to the agents at the annual convention. That year it was being held in Detroit and it was only for four days. We arranged for Jeff's children to stay with Penny and for Mom to stay with my kids. I was looking forward to spending some time away with Jeff in the hopes that he would go back to being happy for awhile. I didn't know what his problem was, but being around a depressed person was getting very depressing.

Colleen was also taking her husband Ryan and the guys seemed to get along pretty good. We expected that it would be a good time for all of us. They would be able to hang out together while we attended our meetings. For the trip down there I had worn a T-shirt type dress that had a cutaway waist with rings holding the skirt and top together. When our Executive Manager, Kay saw me in it she asked if I would model the new lingerie line for the agents back home at the local fashion show. She said that she thought that anybody who could look good in that dress would look good in the lingerie. I had never done anything like that before, but it sounded like fun, so I agreed after she told me that they were hiring a professional model for the more risqué items and she would have a bottle of courage in the dressing room for us.

We all enjoyed most of the weekend and the new line was fabulous. I couldn't wait to get home and start showing it to my regular hostesses. The showing of the line was held on the last night and there was a big awards dinner before that, with plenty of wines being served. I guess Ryan had a little too much. Shortly after Jeff and I returned to our room there was a knock on the door.

I opened it to find Colleen in tears with the shoulder of her dress ripped. I hurried her into the room and asked her what had happened. She said Ryan had been freaking out at her about something and had hit her. She had tried to leave the room and he had grabbed her dress, ripping the shoulder. She ran to our room to ask if Jeff would go and talk to him, try to calm him down. She was afraid to go back there alone. Jeff said that he would see what he could do and told Colleen to stay with me until he got back.

Jeff didn't come back until a couple of hours later and he appeared to have done some more drinking. He said that he and Ryan had gone down to the bar for a couple of drinks and Ryan had calmed down, so Colleen left and went back to their room. She was barely out the door when I started wishing Jeff hadn't returned. It seemed that Ryan had put some stupid idea in his head that Colleen and I were conspiring against them.

I didn't know what we were supposed to be conspiring about. Jeff just began to yell and call me names, not making any sense at all. To this day I still don't know what the hell it was all about. I thought they just drank too much, but both Colleen and I decided that we would never take them to a convention with us again.

A couple of days after we got home, we were scheduled to hold the local fashion show. When we did the dress rehearsal and I saw which pieces I was expected to model, I was a little apprehensive. Kay and I appeared to have a different idea of what was risqué, but when she told me that she had a body stocking that I could wear under them, I agreed. When I arrived in the dressing room the night of the show I found that Kay had bought one bottle of wine for all of us. Since there were five models I thought a case would have been more my idea of courage. I had a glass of wine and proceeded to dress in the first item that I was to wear.

It was a beautiful long red gown with black lace trim on the bodice and a red ruffle on the bottom. It was form fitting and I felt wonderful in it, but when Kay told me that I would be the first model on the runway, I needed another glass of wine. I was just standing around waiting, when suddenly Kay came in and told me to go. I didn't have time to get nervous again and made my way gracefully down the runway.

The audience consisted of agents, their spouses and hostesses and there were about a hundred people attending. When I got to the end of the runway I saw that Kay's husband Gary had set up his camera to take pictures. He was having a problem getting the camera to work and kept telling me to stay where I was at the end of the runway. It seemed like an eternity and plenty of time to get nervous again, but it was probably only a minute or two. I just wanted to hightail it back to the dressing room.

The rest of the show ran smoothly and the audience enjoyed the show as much as the models did. I could see that the new line was definitely going to increase our sales and in turn, our commissions. Much as I enjoyed the fashion shows, it took a lot of energy and I was glad to get home for a good night's sleep. I was on a natural high, so sleep would likely be difficult and morning would bring a lot of work getting ready to market the new line.

My high spirits were soon dampened though. There was a psycho bitch in town and one night, to our surprise, Jeff's wife Penny showed up outside our front window with her daughter Teresa in tow. Penny was obviously very drunk and calling for me to go outside. I couldn't believe that she was coming after me and was very tempted to go right out and flatten her.

All the children had been woken up by her yelling and were watching upstairs at their windows. I suppose she was mad at me because Jeff had chosen me rather than going back to her and I could see very clearly at that moment why he had made that choice. There she was, drunk out of her mind, with her thirteen-year-old daughter following along behind her and her other children watching at their windows. She apparently didn't think there was anything wrong with that.

Jeff finally yelled out that I would not be joining her on the lawn and if she didn't leave he was calling the police. They left shortly after, so Jeff and I went up to calm the children down and get them back to sleep. I had been very surprised at Penny's behavior, as we had been getting along very well over the past few months. She had even called me several times when she was having problems with her boyfriend or Teresa, to ask me for advice. As far as I could see we didn't have any problems between us, but I guess she just had too much alcohol and decided to blame me for her lousy life.

About the same time my car broke down and I was fed up driving shitboxes, so Jeff and I decided I should lease a newer car. The one I was driving was a Chevy Nova that I had bought from Bruce for three hundred dollars the year before. He had been trying to sell it and I had been having trouble with my Dodge van, so Mom had apparently convinced him that he should sell it to me, as I really needed it. He finally agreed and after driving it for a year or so, I took it to Dad for some repairs. He was still working as an auto mechanics teacher at the time, so I just met him at the school. When he got under it, Dad found that there were several places on the frame where pieces were actually missing and the car shouldn't have been on the road.

Bruce did tell me many years later that he hadn't wanted to sell me the car, but had because Mom told him I really needed it. I guess he hadn't told her how bad a condition it was in.

The next day Jeff and I went to a car dealership and found a nice small car that would be big enough for me to carry my lingerie samples in, but small enough to be easy to drive. It was an 89 Topaz and the one I was getting was gray in color. It wasn't my favorite color, but at that point I wasn't about to be picky. We had to wait for them to do a credit check and a couple of days later they called and told us that we could go and pick it up.

As I was signing the papers the salesman was going over them with me, pointing out the important details and he said that the color of the car was blue. I reminded him that we were supposed to be getting a gray one and he said that they had found some problems with that one. Rather than have me wait for the repairs to be done they were giving me a blue one instead. He must have thought I was worried about the color, but I really wasn't. I was just remembering what the psychic had told me at Darla's party. She saw me driving a small blue car. It was a spooky coincidence if you ask me.

Ironically, at the same time I was getting my new car, Colleen's husband Ryan was looking for a new engine for his truck and it just so happened that the engine from my Nova was the right size. They had an old tent trailer that they wanted to get rid of and knowing that I loved camping, they offered to trade the trailer for the Nova. I thought that was great, as I wouldn't get anything for the car elsewhere.

Mom and Dad had given me their two-man tent, Coleman stoves and the dishes we had used for camping when they sold their trailer, but even that with the four-man tent we had bought, was not enough space for our new family. We made the trade and I looked forward to our next camping trip. Colleen told me that the canvas for the trailer was in bad shape and would probably need a new one, but I figured we could just throw a tarpaulin over it to keep the rain out and it would work just fine.

My new car was great and business was booming. It was so nice to finally have a reliable car to get around in and not have to worry about how I was going to get to my parties. I also had some new agents working under me and had earned the status of Junior Manager, which meant that I was earning extra commission on my personal sales as well as five percent of my branch sales. That also meant that I had a lot more running around to do as I had to help my agents with parties, train them and also attend all the monthly meetings.

I loved my job. I was meeting many new people and at one of my parties I met someone who would become a very good friend. She arrived late and the minute she walked in the door I felt a connection to her. Her name was Tanya and she was the life of the party. At the time I thought she would make a great agent on my team, but I had no idea how important she would become to my personal life. I laughed when it came time for the guests to try on the lingerie samples that they liked and she just dropped her clothes right there in the living room to try on one of the corsets. She decided to buy it and also book a party of her own.

When I went to do her party, I was very happy that she decided to join my team as an agent. Just as I thought, she was a great saleslady. She quickly built up her business and we had a wonderful time doing meetings and fashion shows together. She looked great in the lingerie and was soon modeling for us, as I was too busy once I had earned my new status. She had a fiancé, James and was getting married the following year, so she was anxious to earn extra money for the wedding.

She always spoke highly of James, but there were times that she would call me just to talk when he had flipped out at her about something silly. Like the time that a fire alarm went off in a nearby building and woke him up. He flipped out at her. She called me in tears and I couldn't believe how juvenile his behavior was. I had only met him briefly once and wasn't impressed with how he made her feel, but it was her life and all I could do was be supportive of her and lend an ear if she wanted to talk.

I was having my own problems with Jeff, although it was nothing I could really put my finger on. He had taken over doing most of the cooking since I was doing three or four shows per week. He agreed that he would cook on those nights even though it was usually just hotdogs or hamburgers and fries. He wasn't used to cooking, so his talents were limited, but with time I was able to teach him some simple recipes that the kids enjoyed, so that they could have something healthier and different to eat every day. I wasn't really comfortable leaving him with the kids so much. He pretty much treated my kids like they were an inconvenience. One of his friends told me that it was even more obvious when I wasn't around. He spent money on them and bought them new bikes, but I got the impression that he did it just to try and convince everyone how wonderful he was and to keep me with him.

I really started to feel uncomfortable when I came home one night and found Jen with a serious cut on her forehead. Jeff told me that she had been standing on the toilet, slipped and hit her head on the counter. I took his word for it, as accidents do frequently happen with so many children to watch. Several years later Jen told me that she hadn't slipped on her own. He had grabbed her arm to pull her down off the toilet and she had fallen and hit her head on the corner of the counter. He had spanked her and told her not to be such a baby when she cried. To this day she has a scar almost an inch long on her forehead.

Much as I was feeling uncomfortable I told myself that he wasn't really a bad guy and wouldn't actually hurt my children. They called him Daddy and he loved them. I had to keep working so I could take care of my children when I finally left Jeff, as I was planning to do. I would have to leave him sooner or later, but that would be more difficult with his children also living with us. I loved them and they looked at me as more of a mother than Penny, so I didn't want to hurt them. They had enough problems to deal with being in and out of foster care. At least my children always had me to depend on. Jeff's children had nobody they could trust to take care of them other than me.

Luckily for me, Jeff had quit drinking for a long time and that made it much easier for us to get along. He tended to get nasty when he drank and I had told him that he needed to do something about it. He agreed and stopped for the most part, but drank when we entertained or went to a party, which wasn't often. Even in those situations he wouldn't drink as much as he had previously. I hadn't been drinking much myself, especially at home and was feeling much better about it. It also helped that Jeff always had pot to smoke and I found that much more relaxing than alcohol.

CHAPTER ELEVEN

1990

My Broken Heart

In the spring of the following year I got a call from my brother-in-law, Mitch. He wanted to stop by and see the kids & I. He had some Christmas gifts for us from my mother-in-law, Jean. I wondered why he would be bringing Christmas gifts at that time of year. When he came over he told me that Jean had given them to him to deliver at Christmas, but he had been arrested and spent the past few months in jail. When he was released, he realized that the gifts were still in the trunk of his car.

Before Mitch arrived I told Jeff that he was coming over and the reason for his visit. Jeff seemed fine with it at the time. I hadn't had contact with my in-laws for a couple of years, as they hadn't kept in touch for long after I got involved with Jeff. I had been a little upset about it and figured if they cared to see the kids they knew where to find us.

When I called Jean to thank her for the gifts later, she told me that she hadn't called because she didn't want to interfere in our lives since I was with a new man. I told her that was ridiculous. She wasn't interfering in my life! She was the children's grandmother and had every right to be a part of their lives regardless of who I was with. If Jeff had a problem with it, that was his problem. Jeff had been to her house with me several times and even gone for Thanksgiving dinner when we were first together, so I didn't understand her thinking that way. Maybe they just didn't like Jeff. Either way I had thought it sad that none of them had stayed in touch with the kids.

At any rate, Mitch came over with the gifts and Jeff went down to the basement to entertain himself while Mitch was there. He seemed to be upset about something and shortly after Mitch arrived he went to the store, coming back with a bag that he took downstairs with him. Mitch was busy helping Arthur assemble a toy that Jean had bought him, when about 20 minutes later, Jeff came upstairs.

Apparently, Jeff's quick trip had been to the liquor store and the bag contained a mickey of vodka, which he had polished off very quickly. He was quite drunk and irate. I wasn't sure what he was angry about, but it had something to do with Mitch being there and my involvement with his family. Mitch kept telling Jeff that he had nothing to do with whatever was bothering him. He didn't even want to hear about it, but Jeff wouldn't leave it alone. Mitch didn't stay long, as he didn't want me to have any problem with Jeff because of him. He thought the situation would cool off if he left. He asked first if I would be okay and when I assured him that I could handle it, he left.

After Mitch left, Jeff got angrier and I sent the kids upstairs to play while I tried to get the situation under control. Before long I could see that wasn't going to happen as Jeff grabbed the kids' Nintendo system off the TV and threw it across the room. I ran upstairs, grabbed my kids and left to go to my parents' house. I told Jeff that I would not be back until he had sobered up and cooled off.

I stayed at my parents' until the kids started getting tired and were ready for bed. Several hours had passed and I thought it was enough time for Jeff to have either passed out or sobered up, so it should be safe to go home. When I arrived home I was surprised to find Teresa there. Jeff hadn't spoken to her for several weeks, since she and Penny had shown up on our front lawn. At the time, he had said that she would never be allowed in his house again and yet there she was. Her boyfriend was with her and the three of them had obviously continued to drink, so Jeff was in great shape.

I put my kids to bed and went downstairs to stay out of Jeff's way, but he wasn't going to let it go. He was yelling down the stairs at me, calling me names and both he and Teresa were saying what a bitch I was and who needed me, etc. They kept asking why I didn't just go back to Max's family and leave theirs alone? I was so hurt after all I had done for all of them, that they could talk to and about me that way, but when I looked at who they were I wasn't really surprised.

I wasn't going to put up with it however, so I got on the phone right away to begin making arrangements to move out before the weekend was over. It was Friday and I intended to be out of there by Sunday. I phoned Colleen first, to ask if she would go with me the following day to look for a place and she said that she would be happy to. She would also help me pack and move my things. My parents agreed to loan me the money for last months rent and said that I could pay them back in payments when I could afford to.

The next morning Colleen showed up with $800 in cash for me to borrow until I could get the money from my parents. That way if I found a place while we were out I could pay a months rent right then and there. I hadn't asked her for it and was very touched that she took it upon herself to bring it for me. She was a great friend and I loved her dearly for being there when I needed her. We went out apartment hunting and were lucky to find one that morning that was available immediately. It was a basement with two small bedrooms that the kids could use and I would sleep on the sofa bed in the living room. It would be cramped, but I didn't care. I just wanted to get away from Jeff right then and worry about the rest later.

I arranged for a truck on Sunday, so Colleen and Ryan came to help me pack my things and move them to my new place. Of course, Jeff was in shock as he had sobered up and realized that I was serious about leaving. He went into his old "I'm so sorry" routine. He even helped me move my things and told me that if I needed anything just to let him know. He knew that he was losing me and was doing everything he could to hang on. I realized that I might still need some help from him if I was going to continue my business, so I decided to be nice and let him help me. It was his fault that I was leaving and taking my kids to a much smaller place, so why shouldn't he help me out?

Things were tough once I moved out. I was very distraught at the sudden change in my circumstances and found it difficult to get on my feet. I had allowed myself to depend on someone else to help me and suddenly had to do it on my own again. I was making good money as I had been working very hard. I just wouldn't make the mistake of depending on a man again. I would make sure that I could always take care of myself and not be in a position that I had to put up with any crap from a man. Experience was teaching me that the only one I could depend on was me. I was more than capable of taking care of myself and I really didn't need a man for that. I would never let myself get into a position like that again.

On the bright side, every year the company I sold lingerie for had a promotion where agents could earn an all expense paid trip to the annual convention. This year, the destination was Hawaii. The one place in the world that I had always wanted to go! When they announced it, I cried and decided right then and there that I would go, no matter what it took. I had joked around with Kevin, who by then had become my best friend, about taking him with me. Although, he definitely took it as a joke, in my heart I would have loved nothing better than to have him with me. I had dreamt of going there on my honeymoon. Since I wasn't getting married again anytime soon, I would have settled for going with someone I loved.

****

Mr. Right

Jeff had asked me to marry him several times, but I knew that it wouldn't work out. I was in love with Kevin. At the time Kevin had told me to stop the wedding if he said he was getting married, after I had told him to do that for me. I felt he was just saying that because he was scared of another bad marriage and not because he was in love with me. I had asked him once, "If you could be anywhere right now, with anyone in the world, where would you be and with whom?" He had replied, "I would be on a beach in Mexico sipping Margaritas with you".

"That's really sweet", I said, "But I meant with anyone, including famous people".

"I know what you meant and you're who I would be with".

I had never been happier and looked forward to being able to spend the rest of my life just loving him. That was, as soon as I could be free of Jeff.

Kevin had been my ex-husband Max's roommate when we were first dating and over the years he had been my hero. There had been many times that he had come to my rescue when Max was drunk and out of control and I would always love him for that, among other things.

I hadn't spoken to Kevin for a few days and when he did call he told me that his parents were selling the house he had been living in, so he was staying at his ex-girlfriend Kathy's. The last I had heard about her, he hadn't spoken to her for many months, so I had assumed their relationship was really over.

I was shocked and disappointed, as I didn't know that he had even been talking to her again. He assured me that it was a temporary situation, until he could make other arrangements and only expected to be there a couple of weeks to a month. He said he was not getting back together with her. I wasn't sure I believed that, but it was his life, so

94

there was nothing I could do about it. I was pretty sure then that he wouldn't be going to Hawaii with me.

****

Jeff was doing whatever he could to win me back and looking after the kids when I went out to do my shows. I didn't want him to get the idea that it meant I was getting back with him, but I had no choice. I couldn't leave the kids alone and needed the income to support us. There was no way I was taking him to Hawaii with me and when I realized that Kevin wouldn't be going, I made sure that I only earned enough trip points for one person to go, rather than two.

Jeff understood that I had to go alone and offered to have the kids stay with him while I was gone. I agreed, as once again I had nobody else to take care of them and I wasn't about to miss out on a dream trip. Mom would have taken them, but she still had her own kids to take care of and I didn't want to impose on her any more than I already had.

In July of 1973 my little sister Heather had been born. Because I was only 15, I was still living at home and it was a wonderful thing to have that little bundle of joy in our house. I had always wanted a sister and I loved taking care of her, so I spent much of my time doing just that. Mom was finally able to stay home and be a full time Mom. Dad wanted her to be home rather than having someone else raising their child. I could tell Mom was happy with that arrangement and even though she had moments when she would rather have been somewhere else, she was a very loving mother.

Two years later was the birth of my second baby sister, Monica. Mom's due date was right around Christmas, so we were all a little anxious that she would be in the hospital for the holidays. Monica came into this world Dec. 20, so they were both home for Christmas. She was so precious and I was very happy to have another sister, even though I was no longer living at home by then. I still babysat Heather at the time, so I would have plenty of time to spend with Monica as well. When I was planning the trip to Hawaii, Heather and Monica were still only 17 & 15, so I didn't think Mom would want to have three more kids to take care of.

In the meantime, I continued to work hard paying the bills and was just able to make ends meet with rent, car payment and food to pay for. It hadn't seemed to be that hard before when I was on my own and I was getting very depressed. One of my lingerie hostesses, Jessica was doing jewelry parties and she asked if I would hostess one for her. I thought it sounded like a great idea and she was a good friend, so I agreed. Little did I know then that Jessica was also someone who would help change the course of my life by helping me to keep on the right track. She was psychic and that would be the first of many meetings we would have in my home, although for different reasons.

I scheduled the jewelry party and started calling to invite my guests. I thought it would be nice if I invited Kathy, seeing as Kevin was involved with her again, even if they weren't quite a couple. She said that she would see if she could come and thanked me for the invitation. The night of the party everyone showed up except for Kathy, which didn't really surprise me. We had a great time and the jewelry that Jessica was selling was beautiful. I bought some and got some free for hosting the party. I was happy with the results and so was Jessica.

Within the next few days I called Kathy to find out why she hadn't come. I didn't care that she hadn't, but I was hoping to get Kevin on the phone, as I hadn't spoken to him for a while. I was stunned when Kathy told me that she hadn't shown up because they'd gone to Las Vegas, where they had apparently been married!

I couldn't believe it until Kevin called me the next day and confirmed what Kathy had said. I remembered what he had said I should do if he ever told me he was getting married again, but I hadn't had a chance to say anything about it. It didn't matter who I was trying to have a relationship with, deep down in my heart I knew he was the man for me.

I also remembered who he said was the one person he would be with if he could choose anyone, so I didn't understand, once I was free again, why he had married someone else. I guessed that he wasn't in love with me after all. We had talked about it in the past. What would it be like if we had a romantic relationship? He said that he had thought about it and was afraid that if we tried to have that kind of relationship we would lose what we had now - the most important friendship either of us had ever had.

I could see his point, but I believed that the person you married should be your best friend. It didn't matter anymore, he was married and I knew in my heart that Kathy would get pregnant and he would be tied to her forever. When I spoke to him for the first time after the wedding he laughed when I told him I thought he was nuts to marry Kathy. "What the hell," he said, "I can always get it annulled". I thought that was a great start to a marriage and it didn't indicate that he was madly in love. He told me many months later that he had married her because she kept nagging him to. His reasons were almost as bad as mine had been, but at least I wasn't stupid enough to make that mistake again.

CHAPTER TWELVE

1990

Paradise

Finally the time came to go to Hawaii and I found it hard to contain my excitement. I hadn't been on a plane since I was a child and it was to be a twenty-four hour trip. Once we got there I soon got over my jetlag. I had arrived with $270 in my pocket for souvenirs and whatever extras I needed for the ten days I would be there. We stayed at the Hilton Hawaiian Village on Waikiki Beach and it was amazing.

When Colleen and I went to check into our room we found out that we had been lucky enough to get a mini suite. It consisted of a large bedroom that slept four people, a bar, kitchenette, dressing room and washroom. The balcony overlooked a military base where we watched the soldiers do their morning exercises. What a lovely way to wake up.

Our paid expenses included buffet breakfasts every morning and dinner every night. The only meal we had to worry about was lunch and that was usually just a sandwich or something simple. The meals that were provided were more than enough to keep us full. We didn't have to leave the village for anything as there was plenty of shopping and entertainment right there, but we wanted to explore and went on several excursions by ourselves.

As we walked down the street we were approached several times by men with photo albums filled with pictures of gorgeous, scantily clad Hawaiian men. They were strippers on a cruise ship and were looking for ladies to buy tickets for the midnight cruise one evening, but it happened to be on the night of our big awards dinner. We would have rather gone on the cruise, but we declined.

We found a great flea market on one of the side streets, where we were able to buy souvenirs for our family and friends very inexpensively. We found that the gifts at the village were rather pricey, but we did get a great deal on pearls at the village. There was a jewelry booth that had a small bucket of oysters on the counter where you could pick one for only five dollars. They would crack it open and whatever pearl you got was yours. The first one I kept for myself and it was almost the largest that they grew, so I had it set in a gold ti leaf setting and put on a gold chain. I also got a gorgeous gray one for Mom and smaller white ones for each of my sisters. Black pearls were Mom's favorite, so she just loved hers. My sisters were a little too young to really appreciate theirs, but I hoped when they grew up they would treasure them.

The company we worked with had planned a day trip, which was included in our package, and we spent the whole day away from the village. There were about a thousand of us and some of us chose to leave early and visit the Dole pineapple fields. There was a store where we could buy all sorts of pineapple products and souvenirs. I bought a beautiful set of wooden salt and peppershakers for my collection.

After the pineapple fields, we met up with the other agents at Waimea Falls, which was a huge garden growing all the various plants and flowers that were indigenous to the islands. We could walk through, as Colleen and I chose to do, or take an open-air tour train that was driven along the paths slowly as the driver described the vegetation to the passengers. The final destination was the actual Waimea Falls and there was a cliff diving show scheduled shortly after we got there.

As Colleen and I were waiting for the show to start, we noticed a very good-looking guy picking up trash with a pick. When he looked over at us I said, "Don't you think you should be getting ready?" He looked over at the clock above our heads and replied, "No, I still have ten minutes". I was flabbergasted. I had been joking, but apparently he was one of the divers in the show. He came over and sat down with us. His name was Chuck and he was a native Hawaiian who had been diving professionally for several years. The next thing we knew he stood up to take off his shirt and shorts and underneath were nothing but a very small pair of swim trunks. He was tanned, muscular and obviously took very good care of himself. As he walked away he told me that he would blow a kiss after the first dive and it would be for me.

We watched the first dive that he and two other divers did simultaneously. Then sure enough when he came up from underwater, he blew me a kiss. The other girls found that quite amusing and teased me throughout the rest of the show. It lasted about thirty minutes and they were diving from heights that would have terrified me, doing fancy tricks on their way down. As we were leaving after the show, I looked back and saw that Chuck was waving goodbye. It had been a long walk into the falls, so we decided to take the train back to the entrance. It was almost time for the bus to pick us up for the next part of the trip to the Polynesian Cultural Center.

As we boarded the train, the driver announced a slight delay. We had to wait for one of the divers. Of course several of the agents who knew about my encounter with Chuck were oohing and aahing at me, until we saw that it was the other male diver that we were waiting for. As he neared the train the girls were clearly disappointed that their teasing appeared to be over, until I spoke up and said, "I bet he knows Chuck's phone number though". The diver asked what I had said, so I told him that I wondered if Chuck had a girlfriend and he informed me that he had recently ended a relationship and was currently unattached. He said that he would be happy to give me Chuck's number and wrote it down for me.

When we arrived at the Polynesian Cultural Center, we were treated to a ride in a gondola type boat through winding canals. There were small villages set up to represent the different islands and other boats carrying dancers from several villages, doing their traditional dances. Dinner was included with our tickets at a buffet style restaurant. Tables laden with fresh fruit, seafood and various other native dishes. We stuffed ourselves and were happy to be able to just sit and enjoy the show afterwards. All together there were over a thousand agents and the master of ceremonies dedicated the show to the agents attending. It was a fabulous array of native dances, with a fire show and a medley of Elvis Presley songs at the end.

Between the boat ride and dinner, I called Chuck and he said he would love to see me after the show. As soon as it was over I called him back and told him where we were staying. He said that it was about an hour from his home, but that he would be there soon after I got back. Colleen told one of the other agents, so when Chuck arrived Colleen and Melanie, another one of the lingerie agents, were sitting in our room waiting. Melanie didn't believe that I had actually called him, or that he was coming over and was quite shocked when I answered the door and he was standing there!

I invited him in, but I was embarrassed that the other women were acting like schoolgirls that had never seen a man before. They were giggling, covering their mouths with their hands, so I decided we should make a hasty exit. The bars were open until 4 a.m., so we went down to the bar for a couple of drinks. Later Chuck asked if I wanted to go for a walk on the beach. Well, he didn't have to ask twice. A walk along Waikiki Beach, in the moonlight with a gorgeous Hawaiian man? I was into that!

The beach was deserted and very romantic. We walked for a while then climbed up one of the lifeguard stands to watch the moon shimmering on the ocean. It was beautiful and before long Chuck reached over to pull me close for a kiss. Our first kiss was long and very passionate and I could feel the heat rising between us. We didn't stop there. I did however, stop long enough to suggest that perhaps we shouldn't be up there as it was a lifeguard stand and probably off limits to anyone else. Chuck laughed and said that it should be okay, as he was a lifeguard. Even though I knew that wouldn't matter, since he didn't work anywhere near that beach, I really didn't care. I was lost in the moment.

We made love and it was incredible. His whole body was solid muscle and he seemed to be tireless. Just as I felt a wave of heat rising up from my core, I noticed someone walking along the edge of the water. It didn't matter to either of us, there was nobody else in the world at the moment and I wasn't about to spoil it because of someone I didn't know and would never see again. When it was over, we sat quietly listening to the waves lapping on the shore and whispered softly about our lives.

Chuck told me that he had been asked several times to go and work at Canada's Wonderland, an amusement park only a few miles from my home. They had a mountain there where they also held a cliff diving show. I told him it would be great if he went to work there and we would be able to see each other again. Perhaps he would be the one to help me get over Kevin.

He took me back to my hotel and it was very late by then. He wanted to come and spend the night with me, but I told him that my roommate was a bit of a prude and would definitely not like that at all. He grudgingly agreed that he would come back and see me the next night after work. He had to be back on the cliff top for a 10 a.m. show, which would only give him a couple of hours to sleep once he drove back home. I was excited that I would be able to see him again as we were leaving for home in a couple of days. I went to bed when he left and slept better than I had in a long time.

The following day, Colleen and I went out to do our final shopping as the next day we were headed home. After shopping we went to the beach to try and catch some more sun since we hadn't really had much time for sun tanning and couldn't go home without a good tan. The natives had told us to stay out of the sun between 11 a.m. and 3 p.m., as the sun was very strong at that time. What did they know? It was about 1 p.m. and we wanted to lie in the sun.

I was wearing a bikini and didn't realize until later that the bottoms rode up on my butt cheeks when I lay down on my stomach. We were in the sun for about an hour, half an hour on each side and didn't think that would do much, but an hour or so later we were both beet red. The bottom half of my butt cheeks were burnt to a crisp and soon started to blister.

That evening, we had a formal dinner and I found it very difficult to sit for any length of time, so the dinner seemed to go on forever. Chuck had called in the afternoon and told me that he wouldn't be able to come out again that evening as he was worn out from the night before and from doing four shows that day. He told me that he would love me to call him and keep in touch after I went home and he would let me know if he decided to take the job in my hometown.

I was disappointed, but life goes on and I still had one more night in Hawaii. Colleen and I, along with three or four other women decided to go bar hopping in Honolulu after dinner. We inquired at the hotel about bars with live entertainment and the hotel clerk recommended a place called Studebakers.

It was a very happening place and even though they didn't have a band they did have live entertainment. There was a DJ playing good old rock and roll music and every couple of songs the waiters and waitresses would jump up on the bar and tables and dance for us. There was a dance floor as well and no shortage of partners, as the military base was practically next door. It turned out to be Ladies Night, so drinks for women were only one dollar and they were big drinks. I had several Pina Coladas and one of the other agents ended up drinking thirty-two B52's. We were amazed that she was still upright, but the fact that she weighed over three hundred pounds probably had something to do with it.

Colleen and Heather, one of the other agents, had been talking to a couple of the soldiers for a while and weren't ready to leave when I reached my limit. Joan, Heather's roommate was ready to go, so we left together to go back to the hotel. It looked like maybe the other two were going to hook up with the guys, so we didn't know if we should each go to our own rooms or not. We decided that was their problem and went to our separate rooms. An hour or so later Joan came knocking on my door, asking if she could spend the night there. I told her she could when she said that Colleen, Heather and the two men had gone up to her room and obviously hoped that she would find somewhere else to go.

Colleen came sneaking in just as the sun came up and woke both of us when she tripped over something on the floor. Joan got dressed and headed back to her room down the hall to freshen up and change her clothes and Colleen went right into the shower. I was anxious for her update of the rest of her night and was shocked when she told me what they had been doing. My prudish little roommate had spent the night with one of the guys in Heather's room. Heather had brought the other guy back to the room as well and apparently both couples had their own fun.

Colleen was shocked herself, and apparently had been so drunk she didn't care who was watching. I was upset because she had always made out like she was some kind of virgin, although she had been married and was separated from Ryan by then. I had sent Chuck away the night before when I could just as easily have spent the night with him, except for my concern for her sensibilities, which she turned out not to have.

When she had finished telling me about her night I showered, got dressed and we packed our clothes, leaving them ready for the bellhop to pick up while we went down for breakfast. Our plane left a couple of hours after breakfast and it was a miserable trip home. I cried when we took off because my dream was over and I felt like I would never see Hawaii again. I had a feeling I would never see Chuck again either and he seemed like a great guy. I hoped that someday I would go back there, but that I would be on my honeymoon, the way I had always wanted to see Hawaii.

It had been a great vacation, just not quite the way I had dreamt it would be.

CHAPTER THIRTEEN

1990

Coming Home

When I arrived home, reality hit hard. Jeff and the kids were waiting for me at the airport. I missed the kids and was grateful to Jeff for taking care of them for me so that I could go, but going back to my tiny apartment made it seem like the whole thing had been just a dream. The first few days back were very uncomfortable as I still couldn't sit on my burnt butt and had to spend much of my time lying down on the bed. I had to get back to work though and the new line of lingerie that I had to sell made that much easier. My hostesses were anxious to see it and I had booked several parties before I left.

I spoke to Chuck once or twice on the phone, but the magic of the moonlight on Waikiki Beach was gone and I didn't bother calling him again after the first couple of times. He wasn't moving to my hometown and I couldn't afford the long distance charges, so he soon became just a fond memory that I would cherish in my heart. I often wondered years later if he remembered me at all.

My children seemed to be happy and healthy enough when I got home. Jeff had taken good care of them from the looks of it. I didn't hear any complaints from them and apparently Jeff and my friend Tanya had taken them to Niagara Falls for a day. I was, however, shocked and dismayed to find out that while I was gone Jeff had sent his own children, Jane and Brian back to CAS and they were back living in a foster home. I couldn't believe that he had done that to them.

He said at the time that he had been unable to handle working and looking after them. He hadn't arranged a babysitter for the time that he was at work, but he was usually home by 10 a.m. He had to leave around 4 a.m., so I could see where it might be a problem as they were too young to be left alone. Once I wasn't there to be with them he felt he had no alternative. If I were him, I would have changed jobs before I gave up my children, or tried to find a live-in babysitter. That was just me, but I couldn't understand parents who hit the first challenge in caring for their children and handed the responsibility over to strangers.

I found out many years later that Jeff told his kids that he was sending them back to foster care because I had left him and that I had left because I didn't want to live with them. That was totally untrue, but that's the kind of man he was. Still, I felt somewhat guilty for a while. Had my leaving been his real reason for sending them away? I had to remember that my first responsibility was to my own children and the others were Jeff and Penny's responsibility.

Jeff hadn't been drinking that I knew of since I had left and was still doing everything he could to convince me to move back. In a way I felt that he just wanted to get back together to have someone there to look after his children. In my heart I didn't think he really cared that much about them. He was the kind of person who liked to put on a good show for outsiders. Behind closed doors it wasn't hard to see that he really only cared about himself and what was convenient for him.

He was very generous with his money and had bought my kids new bikes during the first couple of years we were together, but he didn't really pay much attention to them. It felt like he was trying to buy their affection and hang onto me through them. He had even gone out to buy new living room furniture after I left him and had insisted that I go with him to pick it out. I told him it shouldn't matter what I thought of it, as I wouldn't be living with it.

He later told me that his hope was that if I liked the furniture better I would come back. He just didn't get it. It wasn't about material things; it was about his behavior when he drank. I would rather do without some of the things that his money provided if it meant that our relationship would be better. That was more important to me than money.

I found it very tough however, after I got back from Hawaii. Business was good, but I just wasn't making enough to keep up with the bills, as a good portion of my income had to go back into the business. Jeff was still taking care of the kids while I did my shows. They stayed over on the weekends if I had a show because I didn't want to drag them out late at night to take them home. All in all it was hard on them as well and they wanted to go 'back home'. I finally conceded and in the fall we moved back in with Jeff, on the condition that if he ever got drunk and abusive again he would be the one to leave. I was not giving up our home again because he couldn't control himself.

Things went good once I moved back. I was able to relax a little once I got used to being there again. The kids had been bugging me to get a dog and since we seemed to be settling down, I told them I would think about it. I was talking to my friend Jessica and she said that her dog was about to have puppies and offered to give me one.

When I told my sister Monica she asked if she could buy it for them as a Christmas gift. I told her that it was free, so instead she paid for the other expenses, like shots and food, etc. The children didn't know about it until I brought home a cute little puppy one day. It was very cuddly and Jeff decided that he wanted to name him Harley. The kids thought that was a great name. I agreed as Jeff was always telling me he wanted to buy a Harley someday. That became a family joke as he was thinking of something more along the lines of a motorcycle.

The following summer, which would have been in 1991, I worked my way up to manager, which meant an increase in my commissions. I felt bad that Colleen had been unable to achieve that level before me, as it meant that I would no longer be part of her group and she would lose the commissions on my branch of agents. I had been holding back to give her time to get there before me, as she had become one of my best friends and I didn't want to break away from her. But I had to go on and do whatever I had to in order to support my family. Of course, being the friend that she was, she encouraged me to go for it and not worry about what she was doing.

I was having some behavior problems with Arthur at that time. He was getting into trouble at school and they kept asking me to go in to talk about it. When I spoke to Arthur about it he would usually tell me that someone had said something about me, which made him angry and he would hit them or push them to defend me. I explained to him several times that they didn't know me personally and were just saying things to make him angry, not because they believed that I was a bad person. I told him to ignore it and they would stop doing it when they saw that it wasn't upsetting him. It wouldn't be fun for them anymore.

The school called one day and said that Arthur had been too rough with a girl during recess. I found that difficult to believe as Arthur had been raised to never hit a girl. Jen had tormented him since she was old enough to walk and he had sustained several injuries at her hands, yet never hit back. When I questioned Arthur about it he told me that they had been playing a game called "boys catch girls" and the girls had been laughing and running away, all as part of the game. One of the girls had been upset that Arthur had caught her by grabbing her arm and she complained to the teacher. The school however, was concerned about his behavior and wanted to have him see the school psychologist. I didn't see any harm in that and told them to go ahead and set up an appointment for him.

Arthur was seven years old and still wetting his bed almost every night and doctors had told me that there was no physical reason for it, so the cause must be psychological. I had taken him to the hospital for tests to make sure there were no problems with his kidney, bladder, etc. and they had found nothing wrong. While I was waiting for him to wake up from the anesthetic I had written a letter to Max telling him how much I resented the fact that he had not been there for his children. Arthur and Jen had been so young the last time they had seen him that they didn't remember him. As far as the kids were concerned, Jeff was their dad, even though they knew that he really wasn't their father. I had received no response from Max.

When I asked Arthur why he misbehaved sometimes he told me that he was angry with Max and that if Max was bad then he must be bad too. I had never told them anything bad about Max; just that he had some problems that prevented him from being a good father to them and that it was not their fault in any way. I felt at that time that perhaps some counseling would be a good thing for Arthur to help him deal with the fact that he couldn't have the father that he so desperately wanted.

When Arthur went to see the counselor however, it only made matters worse as far as the school was concerned, but turned out better for our family. He apparently told the counselor that I had put seven bottles of cayenne pepper into a glass of milk and made Jen drink it. Fortunately, Susan went to the same school, so they had called her down to talk to the counselor. She told them that it wasn't true at all and that Arthur told stories all the time.

The reality of it was that my grandmother had told me that a good way to teach children not to talk back or swear was to put a touch of cayenne pepper on their tongue when they did and they would soon learn not to. Some may say that it was cruel, but they only got enough to make their tongue tingle a little and it was very effective as my children soon learned not to talk back to me or to swear in my presence.

Regardless, the school felt the need to contact CAS on my children's behalf and before I knew it a worker showed up at my door to speak to me. She spent two hours talking with Jeff and I. At the end of it she told us that she wasn't at all concerned about my children's well being, but she was concerned about the stress that I was under. She asked if I would like to have a child management worker come to visit us and offer some effective ways of dealing with the kids. She explained that it was strictly voluntary and I could stop the visits at any time. I thought it was a great idea and agreed that it might help.

The following week Gary, a CAS worker, came to visit. He visited with Jeff and I first, until the kids came home from school. He was a few years older than I was, with a great smile and eyes that just sparkled. I like him instantly. We set up weekly appointments, which would begin with a meeting at the kitchen table where we would each speak in turn, starting with me. I would explain to Gary what the children had been up to the previous week and he would address my concerns with each of them.

He explained to them that they were very lucky to have a mother that worked hard and took good care of them and that they had to learn that there were rules everywhere that had to be followed. He also told them on several occasions that if they didn't like the rules at my home he could find them somewhere else to live, but they would live with strangers and there would still be the same rules. That seemed to get their attention, as well as learning to put them on 'time out' when they misbehaved and using a reward system when they did their chores or went to bed without giving me a hard time.

Gary worked with a lot of children because of his job. Since I was great at making crafts, over the course of the two years that he came to our house I made several stuffed animals for him to use when he did shows for kids. He had two characters that he used a lot. I knitted him several sweaters with the character's pictures on them and he raffled them off to raise money for underprivileged kids. He also recorded a cassette tape of children's songs and wore his sweater for the cover picture.

At one time when I was having a particularly hard time with Arthur, Gary sat down alone with him and did a psychological profile. At the end of it, Gary told me that Arthur was a very normal child and that he didn't have a malicious bone in his body, but would defend me at all costs. Arthur seemed to benefit greatly from his relationship with Gary and we were sorry to come to the end of our meetings. Gary said that we seemed to have a handle on things and there wasn't much more he could do to help us. He told us we could call him anytime.

During the time that Gary was visiting us, Jen's grades at school improved greatly and she got glowing reports from her teachers. Arthur and Susan's were about the same, but Susan really hadn't had problems in that area and all Arthur's teachers said that he was very bright and just needed to apply himself. Arthur also started playing soccer and we had a great time going to his games. He didn't really do much the first year and I laughed to see him standing with his hands on his hips watching the other players running around after the ball.

He wasn't very confident and seemed to be scared of the ball, but by the second year he improved to the point that they decided to make him the goalie. He wasn't the best goalie in the world, but he wasn't the worst either and he seemed to enjoy that more than running up and down the field. By the third year he pretty much lost interest and didn't want to go to the practices, so he dropped out part way through the season. That was the end of his athletic career as I told him that I didn't have money to waste if he wasn't going to continue throughout the season.

I tried to find something that interested him and he tried Beavers, which was a division of Cub Scouts, but he lost interest after the first year. He was right into it in the beginning, but soon had little enthusiasm when it came time to go to the meetings. I had tried Jen in Sparks, a division of Girl Guides and she also only lasted one year. Susan entered Girl Guides and she seemed to enjoy that for a couple of years, until she discovered boys.

I had been in Pioneer Girls when I was young and had enjoyed the activities and earning badges, so I had hoped that my children would as well, but I couldn't force them. Susan had earned several badges during her time in Girl Guides, but it just didn't hold her interest for long. They didn't seem to care about much of anything, after school sports or other activities. Susan did enjoy Folk Dance Club, but again only for a couple of years.

They didn't have any hobbies to speak of, but would get into doing crafts when I was doing them. I was and still am an avid craftsperson and enjoy many different craft and needlework activities. I tried to teach them to my children as well, but none of the children really took much of an interest. I had hoped that having a hobby would help them find something to care about as I took great pride in creating things. The finishing of a project was always a thrill for me, because I had created something unique and beautiful with my own hands. It was like a meditation for me and helped to relieve a lot of my stress.

I cared about the things that I was creating. The people that became the recipients of my crafts enjoyed them as well and at times were amazed at my talent. It was a great boost for my self-esteem and was for the children when they took the time and initiative to work at something. The problem was that their interest moved elsewhere quickly and I could see that all of them had low self-esteem. I was at a loss as to how to help them and tried to focus on their positive attributes and talents, but there was little that they cared about. Susan and Arthur later enjoyed writing poetry, which was a good thing, but much of their writing was very dark and depressing and that was a bad thing.

Jen did some creative writing at school during her early years, but didn't keep it up outside of school and as she got older she lost interest in that as well. In her late teens she did take an interest in sewing, but by then she didn't have a lot of time or money to pursue it. Arthur turned out to be quite talented at drawing, particularly buildings. I hoped that someday he would use that talent to earn a living.

In the meantime, all I could do was encourage them to keep trying different things and hope that they found something that interested them enough to stick with it. When I looked around at our lifestyle I had to admit that I was probably part of the problem of their low self-esteem. I didn't have much myself. My business made me feel good about myself, as did my hobbies, but my relationships didn't.

Jeff was dealing marijuana at the time and there were people in and out of our house constantly, with the smell of pot permeating the entire house. He must have thought the kids were stupid and didn't know what it was, but I kept telling him that was not the case. I was putting up with it and had to admit that smoking pot helped me deal with my life. I was miserable and the only time I felt good was when I was getting high. I was smoking it on a regular basis as Jeff got home from work early in the day and the kids were at school.

About the only reason I was still with him was because I could get high as much as I wanted. I wasn't stupid enough to not see it. I just didn't have the inner strength to do anything about it. I liked getting high and Jeff had the means to do it, but I knew something had to change. If not for me, at least for my kids. It was not a good lifestyle for them and seeing me living with a man that I didn't love and who made me miserable did not show them a healthy way to have a relationship. It was time for me to move on and get out on my own until I found a man that I could have a healthy relationship with, or be alone.

CHAPTER FOURTEEN

1992

Between a Rock and a Hard Place

I had managed to save some money and could almost afford to pay first and last months rent on a new apartment. Susan was thirteen then, so she was old enough to watch the others kids on the evenings that I had to go out and do shows. I started making plans to leave.

By that time, Jeff had gotten back into drinking, along with smoking pot. One night his friend Roy came over with his girlfriend Bonnie for a few beers. They were going to stay for dinner as it was a beautiful day and Roy had brought some venison steaks to barbecue. I had never tried venison and was very much looking forward to it. Roy had to go to a photo store to pick up some vacation photos he wanted to show us before he started drinking.

Jeff was already half in the bag, but decided to go along for the ride. I was glad to get rid of him for awhile and watched happily as he staggered out to Roy's truck. Bonnie and I made a drink and went to sit in the backyard while the kids were playing video games.

The guys were gone for an hour or so when Roy called and told me that Jeff had apparently been in some kind of a fight and had a broken nose. He was in the emergency ward at the hospital and needed me to take him his health insurance card. I was annoyed that I had to go running to the hospital when I was enjoying a relaxing time with my friend and I was pretty sure that Jeff had done something stupid. Where would he get into a fight going to pick up photos? I figured that they must have gone somewhere else instead.

When I got to the hospital I found out that indeed Jeff

had done something very stupid. He was in a room by then, but still in the emergency ward and the nurses were having a hard time keeping him on a stretcher. He kept trying to jump off and they thought he was trying to get away from them. It didn't take me long to figure out that he was attempting to get to the sink on the other side of the room because he had to vomit. He seemed to be a lot drunker than when he had left the house, but Roy said that he hadn't had any more to drink after leaving the house. He was incoherent, but I got his message when he leaned over and vomited on the floor. That was when I figured out what he had been trying to do.

He calmed down after he had finished, but was very agitated and I assumed embarrassed that he had been unable to get to the sink. The nurses explained to me that he was to be taken down for x-rays and a CT scan to determine the extent of his injuries, but they had been waiting for me to arrive in the hopes that I would be able to calm him down.

They needed him to be still for the tests and he had been very agitated instead. I told them that I thought he would be able to be still and we were off to do the test. I managed to keep him calm enough so they could do what they needed to. Afterwards I went out to talk to Roy and find out exactly what had happened.

Roy told me that he had parked in front of the photo store and gone in to get the pictures, leaving Jeff sitting in the truck. Apparently a guy had come over and asked Jeff to move the truck for some reason and he wasn't able to as Roy had the keys. Jeff got out of the truck and started mouthing off to the guy, calling him names and attempted to kick him.

Roy described the guy as black and 'built like a refrigerator'. He had just come out of the Super Fitness Club next door to the photo store and was wearing a Super Fitness tank top. Roy said that he was solid muscle and seeing that Jeff was about 160-lbs. soaking wet, kicking him had been very stupid. The guy punched Jeff in the face and as Jeff tumbled down, he also kneed him in the face. When Jeff hit the ground he hit the back of his head on the concrete. According to Roy, who had seen the whole thing from inside the store, it took a matter of a few seconds and he thought Jeff got what he deserved. I couldn't believe the stupidity of the man and that sealed my decision that it was time for me to move on. Unfortunately, I would be unable to do so for quite a while longer.

Jeff's resulting injuries were a broken nose, fractured cheek and fractured skull. Within hours of arriving at the hospital he slipped into a coma, where he remained for the next six days. I waited at the hospital until the nurses assured me that there was nothing I could do and there was no point staying there. I called Jane, Jeff's mom and let her know what had happened and she in turn called Penny as the children were back living with her. Jane also told her she didn't think it was a good idea for the children to visit while he was in the hospital. He had a bad case of 'raccoon eyes'; meaning that both his eyes were black and blue, as well his cheek was severely bruised and swollen. He basically looked like a Mack truck had hit him.

The first time I went to visit I was surprised to see that he was under constant watch, as he apparently had tried several times to get out of bed. Although he was comatose for the most part he did have moments of partial consciousness. He didn't understand where he was, or how seriously he was injured.

When I walked into his hospital room and saw a rather large black man sitting at the end of his bed I went immediately to ask the nurses if they knew how he had been hurt. They didn't know the details and I explained what had happened, expressing my concern that perhaps it wasn't the best idea for a big black man to be the first person he saw when he regained consciousness. Little did I know, when he did wake up several days later he would have no recollection of the incident that caused his injuries, or of much else for that matter.

He was suffering from temporary amnesia due to the damage to his brain. The doctor described it to me as similar to what had happened to Mohammed Ali's brain as a result of boxing. Jeff's brain had been severely shaken when he was hit and the front portion, which housed his short-term memory, had been badly damaged. The doctor said that with time he should regain his memory, but at this point he didn't really know who he was or who I was either.

After a few days, when Jeff was able to talk, he said that he knew that I was the woman that he lived with, but had no further recollection of our relationship. He called me "Tandy", although I corrected him several times. He didn't know where we lived and even when I brought pictures to show him, he didn't actually recall the house.

His ex wife Penny was about six months pregnant by her boyfriend at the time and brought the children to see him one day when I wasn't there. Jeff's mother Jane had advised her to wait until he had recovered more from the bruising on his face, but she came anyway. I was very upset that Penny convinced Jeff that they were still married and that she was carrying his child. He had gotten a vasectomy after Brian was born, so that was impossible and they had been divorced for a couple of years by then!

I thought it was very cruel of her to do something like that to him and even worse to get the children to play along. She must not have realized that he would regain his memory eventually and when he did that would be pretty much the end of any friendly exchanges between them. Besides, she was still living with her boyfriend, so I didn't know what she thought she was going to do about that. She couldn't take Jeff to her house and they would most definitely not be staying at our house. That proved to me just how unbalanced she really was, but in the meantime she had also convinced the doctor and nurses that she was his loving wife.

Later that day when I went to visit, I was told that his wife had denied me access to him and I was not allowed to

118

visit. I was furious and called his mother Jane immediately, who in turn called Jeff's doctor. She told them the truth and as she was his next of kin told them that under no circumstances was Penny to be allowed anywhere near him for the duration of his stay there. Once we had that straightened out I was free to visit. It wasn't that I was anxious to, but as I had been his common-law wife for the past six years I felt that it was my duty to at least take care of him until he could take care of himself. I was stuck in a position that I was anxious to be out of, but he was very much in need at that time and I felt responsible to help him get back on his feet.

Over the next few days he gradually regained his ability to speak clearly and although he was unable to retain any new information, his long-term memory slowly began to return. He started talking about his dad, as though he had spoken to him recently, but his Dad had passed away several years before. He seemed to have slipped back into his youth and his memories of that time were very clear. The doctor finally said that there was nothing more they could do for him and he was to be released on the condition that I would be there to care for him twenty four hours a day. He was not to be left alone for at least the next thirty to sixty days, until he had recovered enough to retain new information.

That was just great! I would be stuck with him constantly and unable to work until he had recovered. There went my plans to leave him – at least for the next couple of months and we would have to depend on the medical benefits from his job to pay the bills.

When I took him home he still had no recollection of our house, so I had to show him around and where everything was. He wasn't retaining new information yet, so I usually had to repeat things several times. It was very irritating when he would ask a question. I would answer it and five minutes later he would ask the same question again. I was trying very hard to be patient and understanding, but it was difficult when I didn't want to be with him and I was forced to not only be with him in the same house, but to be with him all day, every day. I also had to be careful that he didn't try to get up on a chair, to change light bulbs for instance, or fall down the stairs. It was like having another child to care for.

He ended up being off work for three months. At least he was much nicer to the kids and I, but he never stopped talking. He would repeat the same stories over and over until I just wanted to gag him for awhile. I must have heard his entire life story at least a hundred times. He gradually regained his short-term memory and was able to once again retain new information, but he never got over the non-stop talking as long as we were together.

It seemed like he was afraid that if he stopped talking he would lose the ability again. When our friends or family would come to visit it was for short periods of time, as they couldn't stand to listen to him constantly. They all shook their heads and were very sympathetic that I had no escape from it unless he was sleeping. My nerves were raw and I was in desperate need of a break.

That summer Kevin was going to Georgia to work for a couple of months and stay with some of Kathy's relatives. I told him that I would love to go on a trip, so Jeff and I decided that when the kids went to camp for ten days we would drive down to visit Kevin. I wasn't looking forward to such a long time stuck in a car with Jeff and told him to make sure that the stereo was working so that I wouldn't have to spend the whole trip listening to him. I said it in a joking way, but I was very serious. If I could have gone alone I would have.

A few days later, we dropped the kids off at the bus that would take them to camp and headed south. For some reason Jeff wanted to go to Nashville to see the Grand Ole Opry while we were down there. I thought it was pretty stupid as it would take us two days out of our way and I was anxious to see Kevin. There was no stopping Jeff though, so we made the trip to Nashville. We drove around the town looking for the Grand Ole Opry and couldn't find it. I told Jeff to stop and ask for directions, but no, he just kept driving around and we ended up leaving without having seen it. As it turned out he hadn't been planning on going inside or anything. He just wanted to see it from the outside. I started to wonder if he really had lost his mind.

While we were in Nashville we did some shopping and I bought my first pair of cowboy boots. We visited the Elvis Presley museum as I was a big fan and we saw many interesting documents showing that he apparently had been a DEA agent. He was supposedly dead by then, but I never did believe that. Our next stop was a visit to Graceland and it was a great thrill for me.

Mom told me that when she was a teenager she had plastered her bedroom walls with pictures of Elvis, so I had grown up watching his movies and listening to his music. I was disappointed that we weren't allowed to take photos inside. The lights from the flash would fade the colours of the upholstery. Still, it was fascinating to walk through the house and see the rooms that were decorated to suit Elvis's taste and to imagine him actually living in those rooms.

My favourite room was upstairs and I believe it was just a leisure room, decorated in animal prints. I would have loved to decorate a room in my home in the same type of décor, as it felt very natural and wild. We were allowed to take photos outdoors and there were horses running in the fields by the stables at the back of the house. At the side of the house was a small private cemetery where Elvis's mother and supposedly Elvis were buried. After Graceland, we headed towards Georgia and spent the night in Tupelo, Mississippi, the town where Elvis was born. In the morning we set off again for Atlanta and Kevin.

The afternoon that we arrived he was working and we made plans to meet up with him that evening. He was staying with Kathy's aunt and uncle, so we were to go there for a drink when Kevin got home. They were wonderful, making us feel right at home, thrilled to have Kevin's friends from Canada visiting.

When Kevin arrived, we sat out on the back porch, having a few drinks and taking photos. I took a couple of Kevin that turned out great and I have treasured them for many years. Later on we went to a Mexican restaurant and sat on a patio eating Nachos and drinking frozen Margaritas. When Kevin paid the tab I was shocked at how inexpensive the evening had been.

The following day Kevin had to work, so Jeff and I entertained ourselves shopping and sightseeing until meeting up with Kevin in the evening. We went to another bar where they had live music. After I had already had three or four beers Kevin bought me a shot. I asked what it was and he told me it was a snakebite. "Trust me," he said, "just drink it". I really needed to learn that when a man said, "Trust me", I should do the opposite.

I tossed back the shot and knew it was a mistake! It was straight whiskey. I could feel the vomit rising in my throat and quickly searched for the washroom, which was on the other side of the very large room. I staggered as quickly as I could and arrived at the ladies room just in the nick of time. I hadn't eaten much that day, but everything that I had eaten ended up in the toilet. I struggled to regain my composure when I was done throwing up, but when I stood up I was dizzy for a few moments.

When I returned to the table to continue the evening I thanked Kevin for the thought, but asked him to please make a mental note for future reference that my first experience with alcohol had been straight whiskey, which had made me vomit. Strangely enough, it still had the same effect and I would appreciate not drinking it again.

Later on we moved to another bar to have a few more drinks. Jeff got into a snit about something. Apparently he had my ex-boyfriend Mason on his mind. I didn't know why his name had come up, but Jeff worked himself into a real tizzy. He got up and left, saying that he was going back to Toronto and I could just stay there. As he drove off I turned to Kevin and said, "What did I just hear? He's going home and leaving me here in Atlanta with you? He might want to give that a second thought. I may never go back home." We both thought it was quite amusing that Jeff thought that would be a punishment for me.

I couldn't think of anywhere I would rather have been than wherever Kevin was. After a few minutes Jeff came back (guess he rethought it), apologizing and blaming it on the alcohol he had consumed. I really didn't care if he was sorry or not, I was there to have a good time with Kevin and Jeff didn't really matter to me anymore. I was just biding my time until I could get away from him.

When it was time to leave the bar, it became obvious to Jeff that Kevin and I were having a great time. It was our last night together and we were ready to keep on partying. Jeff suggested that we pick up some beer and he drop Kevin and I off at Kathy's aunt's house. I could spend the night there and he would pick me up in the morning. It sounded like a very generous offer and I would have loved to spend the night with Kevin instead of Jeff, but we wouldn't have been sitting up drinking all night, so the beer wouldn't be necessary.

Kevin was all for it, but I knew that Jeff wasn't making the offer out of the goodness of his heart. He just wanted something else to hold over my head and I wasn't about to give him that. He would never let me hear the end of it (at least until we broke up). I could still remember the beating he had given me over his jealousy about Kevin. Even though Kevin was much more important to me than Jeff would ever be, I declined the offer. I would do the smart thing and go back to the motel with Jeff.

When we dropped Kevin off I went in to say goodbye to him in private and as soon as we were alone he wrapped his arms around me, kissing me long and slow. My heart just about burst with the love I felt for him. He was disappointed, as was I, that we couldn't spend the night together, but there would be other chances. In the meantime I would miss him until he got back home and we agreed to get together as soon as he got back. By then I should be rid of Jeff.

CHAPTER FIFTEEN

1992

Help!

It was not long after the trip to Atlanta that we moved to the new house, where I had my sewing room. After writing the poem that broke my heart I decided it was time for professional help. I finally got an appointment with the psychiatrist, Dr. Geller. I spent about five minutes in his office and he assured me I wasn't crazy, but recommended anti-depressant drugs and counseling. I had been having terrifying nightmares for the past few months and he told me the medication would help reduce them so that I could sleep. He set up an appointment for the following week, with a therapist named Jasmine and I was looking forward to meeting with her. In the meantime, I filled the prescription for Sinequan that he gave me and hoped that it would help.

A week or so later I had my first session with Jasmine. It was a short one as it was more or less just for an assessment, to see if I really did need help and if she could help me. I liked her right off the bat and she simply asked some questions about my life. I gave her a quick run down of the events in my life as far back as I could remember and she said, "It's no wonder you feel like you're crazy and alone, you're whole life has been a series of abandonment, betrayal and abuse, but you're not crazy." I was very glad to hear that.

During that short assessment Jasmine also told me that the last thing I should be worrying about was how someone else was feeling. If I felt that I needed to end the relationship with Jeff, then I should do so and not worry about what he needed, that was his problem. She said that she would start seeing me every week and see how that went.

As I was leaving she noticed the book that I was reading, one by V.C. Andrews. I had always enjoyed those books and had read every one that the author had written. When Jasmine saw it she asked, "Why on earth are you reading that?" I said I was reading it because I enjoyed the author. "Do you realize that these books are all about abuse and incest?" she asked.

I hadn't really thought about it, but realized that she was right. She nodded and said," I guess I can see why you would read them, you can relate to the stories." I thought that sadly, she was probably right about that also. I looked forward to seeing her the following week, feeling that if nothing else she would be someone I could talk to without judgment or misunderstanding.

That evening when the kids had gone to bed I gathered my courage to sit down and talk to Jeff. I explained to him that I had some things to work out for myself and I couldn't do that with him living in the house, I needed time on my own. I expected an argument from him, but he said that if I needed him to move out for a while he would make arrangements to leave for as long as I needed.

I knew he wouldn't be coming back, but I needed to get him out of the house before I told him that or I knew he would never leave. I had been spending more time than usual in my sewing room in the basement. Jeff told me the following week that he had arranged to stay with my friend Tanya and her husband Gerry. They said he could stay as long as necessary. I was greatly relieved when he packed his personal belongings and drove away.

After Jeff and I broke up my nightmares continued, but every now and then I had a sweet dream rather than a nightmare. My ex boyfriend Mason was on my mind so much he came to me in a dream.

We made love and fell asleep curled up together like we used to and it was very comforting. After a

126

couple of hours he got up to go home, which wasn't so comfortable. He was obviously late home and had a fight with his girlfriend, so he decided to move out.

Just then my alarm went off and I was disappointed that I didn't get to see how the situation turned out.

Along with some odd pain in my groin, my mouth had been very sore for a few days and when I went to my therapy group I dropped in to see the nurse at the center. Her diagnosis was that I had several mouth ulcers, brought on by stress. I remembered having them quite often as a child and Grandma would give me a big orange tablet to suck on that would clear them up in a couple of days. I hadn't had them for a very long time, so I knew my body was reacting to the stress.

After the first few sessions with my therapist Jasmine, she had suggested joining a new group for incest survivors. She felt I could contribute to the group and also benefit from the group discussions. It turned out to be a good idea and I was finding it beneficial. By the time group was over that day, the pain in my groin had subsided, but the ulcers were very sore.

During the group a woman named Nancy told us that her husband had accused a member of her family of abusing her young daughters. She was involved in a complicated custody battle and her husband had custody of the girls. She was concerned that her daughters would think that she had given up and abandoned them and I told her to just keep fighting and doing whatever she could to be there for them. I had always thought that a mother was the one person that would always fight for and protect her children.

I was still upset that my mother seemed so passive about what had happened to me. I had tried several times to talk to her about it, but found it difficult, as she seemed so detached. I knew that she loved me and through therapy was beginning to see that it was because of her own abuse that she wasn't able to be as strong as I wanted her to be. Jasmine had said that for my own peace of mind I just had to accept that Mom was who she was and I couldn't change her. The best thing for me would be to find someone else that I could rely on for comfort and conversation and just love Mom for being who she was. I hoped that by seeing that I had the strength to get help and deal with my issues, Mom would find the courage to do the same and free herself from the baggage.

I seemed to make a connection right away with another woman in the group, Helen. Probably because we had similar childhood experiences with sexual abuse. Like Mom, she had never seen the fondling that happened to her as being abuse. Before group she had been asking me about the book Secret Survivors and said that she wanted to read it.

When I went home I expected to find a message from Jeff, but there wasn't one. He had started counseling as well, at the same hospital that I went to, and said that he would call after his morning session to let me know how it went. I was concerned when there was no message, although I couldn't for the life of me figure out why I was. I felt that perhaps he was angry with me or had done something to hurt himself, but I didn't know why that should matter to me. He wasn't supposed to be my problem anymore. I was just the kind of person who couldn't turn my back on someone who was making an honest effort to do the right thing.

I noticed that since Jeff had moved out, my life was much easier. Everyone was more relaxed and the kids pitched in to help out with the housework. They also decided that they would like to start doing some of the cooking. Arthur and Jen were only six and seven, so still a little young for that, but twelve-year-old Susan did the cooking, with a little help from me. The other two did the dishes. It was great to see them working as a team and getting along so well together.

Life was also much quieter and simpler without people constantly in and out of the house at all hours looking for pot and the phone ringing off the hook. I was able to cut down on my smoking, catch up on my reading, watch what I wanted on TV, and do my sewing and crafts in peace. I had less headaches and stress pains, so all in all it was much better having one less person to look after and nobody to answer to.

When Jeff had moved out I told him to take whatever he wanted. I didn't care about any of it and I didn't know when and if he would be back. I knew that he thought he would and I just let him think that, or he never would have left. I didn't want anything, just my freedom from him. I was earning enough money to pay the rent and bills myself and take care of my kids just fine.

His car was in my name, so I told him that in order for me to change it over to his name, he would have to sign a note stating that after thirty days of his leaving, everything left in the house was mine to keep. He wasn't happy about it, but I needed to be sure that he wasn't coming back every few weeks wanting something else. I gave him thirty days to remove whatever he wanted, so he took his new television, stereo, personal belongings and $6000 cash from the bank. When he signed the note, I signed over the ownership for his car so that he could transfer it to his own name. I wanted to cut all ties with him.

It was not going to be that easy however. He began spending a lot of time down the street at Bruce and Linda's and although Linda was supposed to be my sister in-law and friend, she was discussing my personal business with Jeff. I decided to distance myself from them until they got the message that I didn't want Jeff knowing anything about my life. He had never had much to do with either Bruce or Linda when he lived with me, but once he left he was hanging out down the street at their place and also with Tanya and Gerry. Tanya had become one of my best friends, so I knew she wouldn't discuss my personal life with him. I could trust her with anything.

I had wanted to talk to my cousin Marvin about his sister Lynn. I remembered taking care of him as a baby and in fact had been doing just that the last time his father Hector had molested me. Marvin however, had grown up to be a wonderful young man, handsome and intelligent. I hoped to find out if anything had happened to Lynn and get him to help me convince her to get counseling.

She was only fourteen at the time and still living at home, so I knew it wouldn't be easy. I was very concerned about her safety, knowing that her father had molested three members of our family. Lydia obviously wasn't going to leave Hector and the police hadn't been able to do anything without Aunt Karen to back me up, so my only hope was that Lynn would get help to deal with whatever happened. I had mentioned to my sister-in-law Linda that I wanted to contact Marvin and the next thing I knew Jeff called Marvin and told him to call me. While I was glad to hear from Marvin I was pissed that Jeff had interfered. I was quite capable of contacting him myself.

I found out that shortly after Jeff had moved out, he and Bruce had gone out to a strip joint and taken pictures with several strippers. He had made sure that word got back to me about it and "how amazing they were", via Linda. That pretty much sealed the fate of our relationship if there had ever been any chance for him. I was relieved actually, as I really didn't care what he did, but he had only done it in an effort to hurt me while professing undying love. That fact really drove home his true colors and his need to play with my emotions, but he could play that game alone. I would never again have a romantic relationship of any kind with him.

We were in a state of truce then and I figured his interest in the kids was only to stay connected to me. After we broke up a couple of his friends told me that when I would go out and leave the kids with him he behaved like they were in his way and was not very nice to them. Many years later I would find out from the children themselves that he had indeed hit them when I wasn't around, but they had been afraid to say anything. I learned to start listening more to my gut and my children after that.

CHAPTER SIXTEEN

1992

The Deep Tentacles of Incest

I was finally able to hook up with Marvin and talk to him about Lynn. He told me that he had put a lock on her bedroom door to offer her some protection from their father. He did feel that she needed protection since both he and his younger brother Mitchell had moved out of the house. He had only stayed there as long as he had so that he could be a buffer between Lydia and Hector. I thought that was an awesome responsibility for such a young man to take on and it shouldn't have been necessary.

I gave Marvin a copy of Secret Survivors to read in the hopes that he would understand the magnitude of what had happened to his sister and how it would change her life. He said that he hadn't told me sooner about Lynn being molested because according to his parents, I was "psycho". Hector was a pedophile and I his victim. Apparently the fact that I spoke out about it made me a psycho? What a messed up family.

They must have thought I would make more of a fuss about it if I had known Lynn was being molested. I had done all that I could do, so what was the difference? Lynn was young and still living at home, so she wasn't likely to go to court and corroborate my story and nobody else seemed to care. I had already told the police, so what more did they think I could do?

One of the detectives had actually told me if it were him, he would distribute flyers in all the mailboxes in Hector's neighborhood. I told him I thought that was illegal. He winked and told me "it is if you get caught". I still didn't have the courage to do it though. Whether he was present or not, Hector still scared me.

Marvin said that he would read the book and get it back to me as soon as possible. When he did a couple of weeks later, I couldn't believe how casual his attitude was. He said he found the book pretty brutal, but that he didn't believe half of it. I told him that as a victim myself I could assure him that every word of it was true and that it was brutal. As I had read the book it had felt so much like my life and feelings that I could have sworn someone had written it just for me.

It didn't sound like Marvin was going to be much help in convincing Lynn to come forward on her own and report Hector, so it looked like it was up to me to try and convince her to get help. I bowed my head and prayed to God to give me strength and guidance and the answer that I got was that I had to try again to have Hector charged and convicted and with any luck, sent to jail for a very long time. Perhaps now that Lynn was older than when I had gone to the police the first time, she would gain courage to speak out when she found out I was talking to the police and decide to come forward too. I felt that would help her to take back her power and perhaps have a more normal adult life than I did.

Aunt Karen told Aunt Mavis that I wanted to let the family know of my intentions and that wasn't true at all, other than Marvin and Lynn. I really didn't care if any of them knew or what they thought of it. By that point they could all go straight to hell for all I cared. My only concern was Mom as I figured she would catch heat from the family for my "bad behavior in speaking out again". We were supposed to be sweeping it under the rug after all.

I was also concerned about Grandma finding out that I intended to go to the police, as she was very ill at the time. I was sure she and Grandpa thought it was all over just because Grandpa said so. I was still very angry with him for his lack of support when he found out about what Hector had done. It was like he was taking sides and had chosen Hector's. I didn't care what he said anymore. He was no longer the boss of me.

Mom had recently told my grandparents about what Hector had done. She hadn't meant to, but had been at their condo and they had been going on and on about what a hard life Hector and Lydia had and how they needed constant help financially. Mom jumped up and said that she was sick to death of hearing about Hector and Lydia and told them what he had done to Karen, Julie and I.

Grandma had spoken to me afterwards and hadn't mentioned it. She had just told me that I had always been her favorite (I found out later that she said that to all her grandchildren) and that she loved me very much and was proud of me. Grandpa, on the other hand, told me that they had spoken to Hector. He assured them that we were his only victims and that it would never happen again. Grandpa told me that I should just forgive and forget. "After all", he said, "you're fine aren't you? And Jeff doesn't think badly of you does he?"

"Why would anyone think badly of me?" I thought, "I didn't do anything wrong, I was a child! And no, I was not fine!" I didn't think I would ever forgive my grandfather for that.

When I told Karen that I was going to the police again she said that she would talk to them this time, once she knew that he had molested Lynn as well. Again I was upset that she wasn't prepared to talk to them when it was just the three of us that she knew of, like we weren't important enough or something. I hoped that by us speaking out and letting her know that there were other victims Lynn would have the courage to come forward herself and get into counseling as well. Mom and Bruce both said they were behind me one hundred percent and also hoped that this time we would be successful in having Hector put away for a very long time.

I was very nervous about having to speak to the police again, bringing it all back up and was anxious to get it over with. I knew it was something that I should have pursued more diligently five years earlier, but I had been so alone then. This time I had support from some of my family, which meant the world to me. It also occurred to me that at the time I had filed my report Lynn was nine years old, so there would at least be a record of the investigation already with CAS and if so, I couldn't believe they would leave her in the house. I reported it before, but really hadn't been sure that she was being abused until Marvin had told me recently. Of course, their finding then was that she wasn't, but knowing what I had learned about pedophiles in families, I knew the odds were great that she was.

My immediate family and Karen's were very angry with Lydia for staying with Hector, knowing what he had done. I believed then that she had known what he was doing to Karen and I back when it was happening and was just in denial.

How could she not know? There were times she was only a few feet away in a tent trailer. Asleep? Maybe, maybe not. I felt sorry for her until I remembered that she had told me that she wanted out and I had taken her to Legal Aid. I had offered her my help and given her advice about how to get away from Hector and all she really had to do was encourage Lynn to tell the truth and the law would have dealt with him.

Instead she had protected and defended him and worst of all, stayed with him. She and the kids would have been safe if she had done the right thing. He would have been in jail. Once Marvin and Mitchell left home there was no kind of protection for Lynn. They certainly were no match for Hector, but at least there were more eyes watching. Lydia could barely walk up and down the stairs, how could she keep an eye on anyone and would she if she could? She hadn't said anything about it when it was happening to Karen and I.

CHAPTER NINETEEN

1992

The Nightmares

Even though I was angry with Jeff for interfering in the situation with Marvin, he was still seeing the kids. One day I called him to see if he was still coming to Jen's swimming lessons as he had told her he would. He was down the street at Bruce's and said that he couldn't go as he had important things that he had to take care of. I found that odd as he had told me the day before that he was going with us. He never wanted the kids to think he was like their father Max, saying he would do something with them and not showing up.

I asked Susan what she thought about him not going and she said it reminded her of Max, so I decided if he let any of them down again I would put a stop to it. I wasn't going to let him jerk them around like Max had done to Susan after my separation from him. It wasn't fair to them.

After the swimming lessons Susan called Jeff to talk to him about the Guns n' Roses concert they were going to, as she was worried that he would cancel that too. He was still at Bruce's, so it appeared that his important business was sitting around drinking and smoking pot with Bruce.

Once again I was having nightmares and one night I was woken by a horrible one:

I let someone into my house for a delivery or something. It was a couple and the man raped me. Jeff came home and I told him about being assaulted, but not that I was raped. He went to the police and confessed that he had stuck a needle in my chest and broken my leg in two places, even though I was still walking on it. He also told them his friend Gord had raped me months before, although I had no memory of it. My brother Bruce went and told my mother that his friend had raped me and he hadn't stopped it. Mom and Jeff went to the police without my knowledge and told them a doctor had admitted to them that he had also raped me, although I had no memory of that either. Neither of them told me until I was getting ready to go to the police station myself. On my way I stopped at a store and ran into Gord, but was unable to express any anger towards him. The whole story was due to be aired on TV before I had even been to the police.

At that point I woke myself up. None of it had made any sense, but it left me feeling very upset.

The next day Jeff called to argue with me about not attending Jen's swimming lessons. Susan had apparently told him he was behaving just like Max and I really didn't see much difference as far as the kids were concerned. He told me that he hadn't been making excuses, he had gone and done what he had to do and gone back to Bruce's. What he didn't know was that Linda told me that he sat there the whole time and hadn't left at all. On top of everything else he was lying to the kids and I again and expecting to get me back? He wanted to argue about it, so I just hung up on him. I didn't have to put up with his crap anymore.

The kids talked to him later when he called back and they asked him why he had lied. He told them, finally, that he had been drinking and didn't want to drive. They didn't have a problem with that, but they did have a problem with him lying about it. Not wanting to drive when he had been drinking was responsible, even if drinking when he was supposed to go out with the kids was not and he shouldn't have lied about it.

I had another bad dream that night, but the bits and pieces that I did remember didn't make any sense.

I had to take blood from my arm, put it into some sort of machine, add something to it and inject it into my arm. All the while the kids were skating in a field.

I was getting concerned about all the weird dreams I was still having and hoped that they would stop soon. I had another group therapy session the following day and ran into Jeff on my way into the building. I ignored him until he called out to me, as I really didn't want to hear anything he had to say.

When I left group he was outside talking to some guy and having a smoke. The kids had asked him to come and visit, so he showed up shortly after I arrived home. Arthur and Susan talked to him for a couple of minutes, and then took off downstairs to watch TV. I called them back up and told them that they had invited him to come over, so they should visit with him. I certainly didn't feel like entertaining him. They didn't really seem too interested once he was there either.

Before he left he tried to start another argument with me about the swimming lessons, determined to get me to say that it was okay for him to lie. I told him that I didn't want to have a relationship with a man that lied, especially when there was no reason to. How was I supposed to trust a liar? I told him that if he just wanted to argue every time I saw him he could just pick the kids up from then on and take them out somewhere instead of visiting at the house. He said, "Then I guess I won't be seeing them".

I would have been just as happy to have him not see them either as I didn't feel like he was a positive influence in their lives, but I had to let it be their decision unless he got to be neglectful or abusive. They were starting to lose interest in seeing him and I thought they were feeling that he really didn't care about them, so why should they care about him? Even though Max was their father, Arthur and Jen had been too young when we separated to even remember living with Max. Jeff was really the only daddy they had ever known.

He wasn't a very good one and I felt they would be better off without him in their lives.

I had another bad dream that night, about Jeff. I didn't remember anything other than the fact that he was trying to lay a guilt trip on me about something. In reality he did that a lot.

I was awakened when Arthur came downstairs to tell me he was having a bad dream. In his dream Daddy (meaning Jeff) had killed Susan and was trying to kill him too. I was very disturbed that a child his age was having such horrible dreams, so I told Arthur to climb in bed with me and we both went back to sleep. I was feeling more than ever that it might be time to cut off contact between Jeff and the kids if they were having bad dreams like that.

When I went to group the next day I didn't run into Jeff as usual. Of course when he decided to go for counseling himself, of all the places in the city to do so, he had to choose the same place that I went. Not only that, he had scheduled his appointments around the same time as mine so that he would "accidentally" run into me. He told Linda that he didn't feel like going to his group that day because all the people there were 'really screwed up'. I thought it was hilarious that he would think other people were screwed up and he was normal.

****

Grandma Benson

My maternal grandmother had been admitted to hospital a few times over the past few months for various problems. When I got home Mom called to tell me that Grandma was in really bad shape. Her potassium was at 6.9 and the doctor told Mom that a level of 8.0 was fatal. She was back in the hospital and not expected to come out again. I guessed she had given up and just wanted to go home and be with her God. I would be very sad to see her leave this

139

world, but glad that her suffering would be over. She had a stroke a couple of months before and had been getting worse ever since. She was in and out of hospital and it had been very difficult for Grandpa, who wasn't in the best of health himself. Mom, Aunt Alice and Aunt Mavis had been helping out as Grandma needed twenty-four hour care and Grandpa couldn't do it all alone.

The next day Mom called again and said that Grandma wasn't responding to anyone, except when they tried to give her medicine, and then she would respond with displeasure. They asked Mom how the family felt about life support and how far they should go to keep her alive. Mom told the doctor that as far as she and her siblings were concerned they shouldn't do anything heroic, just keep her comfortable. I felt that they should let her go whenever she was ready and that she was fighting the medication because she was ready and didn't want to take it.

Nana, Dad's mother, had been like that the previous year and when she stopped eating and taking medication she died shortly after. I had been devastated at her funeral, not so much because I missed her, but because my maternal grandparents had been sitting right in front of me. It wasn't that I didn't love her too; I just hadn't been very close to her. Grandma Benson had been more like a mother to me. With her on the verge of dying I was glad that I was taking anti-depressants, as they would make it easier to get through the grieving process. I felt that when she died I would lose the one person in the world who had always made the child inside of me feel loved and wanted.

I had learned so much of the good I had inside me from Grandma. She always had the time to comfort, teach, help, talk and always told me how very special I was to her. I always thought, especially since having my own children, that she must have the patience of a saint. I remembered that whenever one of us kids fell and skinned a knee, she would get out the bottle of Mercurochrome and draw a happy face over the cut to make us smile, then give us a big hug and comfort until we felt better. As I wrote about her in my journal it was very upsetting, I had been worried that my medication was only helping to repress my emotions and I was happy to find out that I could still cry. Thankfully, by the grace of God, she did recover enough that she was able to go home a few weeks later.

CHAPTER EIGHTEEN

1992

Soul Searching

I was doing a lot of soul searching and trying to find out who I was, once I had the chance to be myself and not have to answer to anyone else. I was reading a book written by Gloria Steinem called "A Revolution From Within". She talked about writing to help heal ourselves and making notes of dreams and feelings as a way to find our inner selves. I found that keeping a journal was very therapeutic for me. It made me look more closely at myself and feel good about who I was.

I walked down memory lane at times, reminiscing about people and significant events in my life, some good, some very bad. Sometimes remembering the past helped me to deal with my children's issues. I remembered as a child, having a bedwetting problem. I would dream that I had gone to the bathroom and was sitting on the toilet. How could I get angry with my child for having the same problem? I had outgrown it and I was sure that Arthur would too.

Later I remembered the bad dreams that I was having as a child and some of them sounded so foolish. But at the time they were very frightening. I had a recurring dream about a shark in a grocery store that was one of those that really terrified me.

A group of people, including several members of my family, was trapped in a grocery store full of water with a great white shark. Jen was with me in the store, but I couldn't remember who else. We tried to make a steel wall with shopping carts; we were on small boats, from which we were fishing. There was an added danger from a tiger trapped in there with us.

I woke myself up that time, but having dreamt it before I knew my family and I did get out, but several others were eaten. I would stay up for a few minutes to shake off the dream, but some nights I would fall back into a different dream and that was one of those nights.

I was trapped in a small variety store with seven or eight people being held at gunpoint by a young man in his twenties. Jen was with me again, but very young, about a year or so. The young man, during the time of our captivity, shot and killed one man who tried to jump him, and the owner, who tried to call for help. One man escaped out the front door. Our captor saw that I was very upset and asked me why I was so scared. I told him that I was scared for my baby and that my grandmother had died that day. He was very sympathetic and told me not to worry, that he would not harm my baby or me. He seemed to relate to Grandma passing as he told me that he had loved his grandmother very much too. Then he sent me to another store to return a video for him and he timed me as I went. I returned the video and ran across the street to buy a small pack of cigarettes. When I came out he was there with one of my sisters and they were putting on overalls. She said he was making her go with him to rob a bank or something.

My alarm clock woke me up from that one.

I felt really dragged out after such a busy night of dreaming, but I had group every morning and the kids had school. The dreams left me shaken and I recalled having some so vivid that I would wake up and have a hard time accepting that it hadn't been reality. I had dreamt a couple of times that someone was chasing Mom around her house with a knife. I had several dreams about Mom dying and some of them were so real that I would call her the next day to make sure that she was okay. I didn't tell her why I was calling, just to check in and see how everyone was doing.

No matter what kind of night I had, there was business to be taken care of. While attending counseling I still had to support the kids and deal with the stresses of everyday life.

Jeff came that day to pick up his clothes and the rest of his things. He was friendly enough, but kept trying to poke his nose in my business. He noticed that I had a new stereo (I bought for $100) and started asking me about money and making snide comments. I ignored him and didn't even let him get to me again. What I did with my money was no longer his business, or where I got the money from.

His mom called me later in the day to say that she hoped the kids and I would keep in touch with her as she considered us family. I told her that we would come to visit them in Cambridge when the weather got warmer. I never did talk to her again; neither of us bothered making the call.

CHAPTER NINETEEN

1992

Thank God for Therapy

I was trying to quit smoking, but decided to start again as I was finding that my nerves were too raw to deal with everything. I was also trying to be patient with the kids as it wasn't their fault and they even asked me to start smoking again so that I would quit snapping at them. I was so angry at the situation, but they also weren't being little angels either.

My sweet baby Jen had once told my old roommate Katy that she misbehaved sometimes "just to see how loud Mommy can yell". Our CAS worker Gary said that Jen had a need to make sure that everyone around her was anxious and tense, and then she felt comfortable. All of that, mixed with my raw nerves, was sure to set off an explosion and I was afraid of losing control of myself.

Then there was Jeff, calling to cry the blues about how my behavior was hurting him. I told him that I didn't want to hear it anymore, to get over it and leave me alone. I didn't love him and there was no way we were getting back together. I was feeling like I had the weight of the world on my shoulders and I just wanted to end it all. I felt like I would seriously lose my mind if something didn't give soon.

Jeff called around dinnertime one night and said he hadn't called earlier because he had been too upset to talk to anyone. We talked for a while and I told him that he had to give up the expectation of us getting back together; we would never again be more than friends. I didn't want to lead him to believe otherwise and seeing him made me feel guilty, pressured to resume a relationship with him. I said that he could see the kids, but that I wouldn't be spending time with him anymore if he couldn't accept that we were just friends. I didn't wish him any harm, I just wanted him to leave me alone and get on with his life. I was glad to be alone with my kids again after we broke up, but it would be a long time before I heard the last of him. I should have paid attention to the red flags in the beginning, especially when I first met him.

By the end of the conversation I heard more or less what I had been expecting. If there was no relationship with me there would be none with my children. This from a man who claimed to love them so much. He said that wasn't what he meant, but that he had signed up for a package deal and without me it was only part of a package. Still, he had been their father for six and a half years, the only one daddy Arthur and Jen had any memory of. That showed me how little he had really cared about them as individuals.

I had only been trying to stay on his good side until the thirty days I had allowed him to move his things out expired. I felt that since I had gotten rid of all of my furniture to accommodate his, I should at least get to keep some of it and I couldn't afford to replace all of it at one time. He said that he was leaving the majority of it because he loved us so much and wanted us to be comfortable. But I knew better.

He really was two-faced and he was only leaving it because he thought that would get him back in the door. He kept saying that he loved me unconditionally, but I kept telling him that he couldn't say, "I love you unconditionally, but only if you're nice to me", that was putting a condition on his love. The thirty days would be up in eleven days, so I told him I would think about the situation.

Kevin finally got me on the phone the following day to let me know he would have the money I had loaned him the next weekend as he had received his income tax return. We talked for a while and when I told him that the counseling was helping me rebuild my self-esteem he said that he always thought I had lots of confidence. He had talked to his doctor about getting some counseling himself, but told Kathy that he was trying to get into anger management. What he really wanted was to figure out why he kept getting mixed up with women like her and stop it. He said that they really had nothing in common and there wasn't much to hold them together. Perhaps my dream would come true sooner than I had expected.

That evening I had to drop by my sister in law Deirdre's to pick up fabric for some clothes I was making for her. I had finally been able to start the dressmaking business I had dreamt of having. It was only part time, but it was going very well and I loved Deirdre's taste in clothing and fabric, so sewing for her was a pleasure and getting paid to do it was even better. I enjoyed getting together with Deirdre and having a chance to see Natasha once in a while.

She was having a hard time since Bruce and Deirdre had split up a couple of years before, but Deirdre had her in counseling. Bruce had lived with Linda after that, so it had been another new situation for Natasha. I finally got the chance to talk to Deirdre about why she had chosen to leave Bruce at that particular time. I had always had a bad feeling about it and had heard several rumors. So I wanted to get it right from the horse's mouth.

What I knew was that Bruce had lived up north with our biological father George and our little sister Katy was about thirteen at the time. All of a sudden Bruce had come back to the city and wouldn't talk about what had transpired between him and George, but I could sense that it was something bad. Why else wouldn't he talk to me about it? We had our differences, but we had been close enough to talk about important issues in our lives. He also would not discuss the issue of sexual child abuse when I tried to talk to him about what happened to me. He had talked to me about it when I first told him about Hector, but since then he avoided it whenever I brought it up.

When I talked to Deirdre that night she told me that she had been planning on leaving Bruce for a while. I could see where his drinking could be a problem for her if he was still doing it as much as he used to. She told me that she got a call one day from my father George's wife. Deirdre said she was using what Leslie had told her as grounds for their divorce. Something serious had happened, for which Bruce had been in fear of going to jail. She didn't know why he hadn't.

Bruce had mentioned that situation to me a couple of months before, but he said that the accusations were false. I would find out the truth many years later, but at that time, it made me very uncomfortable to be around my brother. According to Deirdre, Stella had also divorced my youngest brother Doug for some reason concerning George. Leslie herself was currently in the process of divorcing George, which was why we figured she had called Deirdre about the situation with Bruce.

I wanted to believe in my brother, but there was no way for me to know if what I heard were true. I remembered Bruce often making inappropriate sexual comments to me. I couldn't believe that he could say such things to me and he seemed to think it was normal.

I also remembered a night at my house during a party when I reprimanded both Bruce and one of his friends for the way they were talking to our youngest sister Monica and her friend. She was about seventeen at the time and had come to me because they were making lewd remarks to her. I straightened them out and they were well behaved for the remainder of the party.

I knew from experience that Bruce had no respect for females, so I had a bad feeling about it. My relationship with my brother, after hearing that news, was never the same. It wasn't that I stopped loving him; I just didn't go out of my way to be around him. I prayed that someday I would find out none of it was true.

Deirdre had taken Natasha to counseling to help her deal with the separation from her father. Certainly she had other issues to deal with as well, so Deirdre just wanted to make sure that she had someone she could trust to talk to about them.

I had to recognize that being uncomfortable around my brother could be a result of me being abused. I was trying not to paint all men with the same brush as Hector, but it was very difficult at that point. I had always made sure that neither of my daughters was ever alone with Hector by telling them what had happened to me. I didn't go into detail, but I warned all of my children to be aware of the people in their world. Not to fear them, just to be aware of them and scream bloody murder if anyone ever dared to try to take advantage of them. They were pretty street smart and I knew they would come to me if anything ever happened to them.

Fortunately I had a session with Jasmine in the morning. I was feeling very anxious and disturbed by the conversation with Deirdre and needed to talk to someone about it. It wasn't the kind of thing I could talk to just anyone about. My sleep that night was disturbed again by bad dreams, although when I woke up I couldn't remember what the dreams had been about and they left me feeling very tired.

When I went to see my psychiatrist he told me to increase the dosage of Sinequan to two capsules per night and that should help with the restless nights and bad dreams. My session with Jasmine went well and she said that I seemed to be less defensive. She saw a big improvement since I had seen her two and a half weeks previous and I told her about my dreams. She said that the common thread was victimization and feeling trapped, which made perfect sense to me. Most of my nightmares were about me being trapped somewhere, or chased by someone. Even during the day I felt trapped, especially when Jeff just kept "popping" up around me.

I also told her about my conversation with Deirdre and it was very emotional talking about it. Jasmine told me that she thought it was very hard for me to work through things because it seemed every week or so, when I got a grip and started feeling stronger, another disclosure was made to me that set me back. We made another appointment for the following week, instead of the usual two weeks and she asked if I would be interested in a 'cognitive therapy' group. Basically what that would do was help change my thinking to a more positive mode. To be able to recognize irrational thoughts and change them to more rational ones through self talk. I told her I would attend if it was held during school hours and luckily it was. I was pretty quiet during group that day, unable to talk about my life right then. Maybe I would ready be in a few days.

CHAPTER TWENTY

1992

The Circle of Abuse

I wasn't the only one in the family having problems. Aunt Karen had been calling me more often than usual in the past few weeks, to talk about her problems. One day she called because she needed to talk about her marriage again and all I could do was encourage her to get counseling and recommend that Mike do the same. It was definitely helping me with my issues. She and Mike were having marital problems because he was drinking far too much and when he drank he became verbally abusive, calling her names, etc. She would react by being cold towards him and when he sobered up he would apologize and the circle would start all over again.

It was easy to see why he would have a drinking problem, being the child of an alcoholic parent. The after effects were much the same as with an incest victim. But as an adult he still needed to be responsible for his own behavior. His father had died of a heart attack either right before or right after his birth, I was never sure which, and his mother had drowned her sorrows in alcohol. Mike had been verbally abused by her his whole life. He refused to seek help because he didn't think any of his past experiences were causing problems in his life. I knew from my therapy that he was dead wrong about that. The things that had happened to me as a child had a huge impact on my adult life.

During our conversation Karen also told me that she had spoken to Lydia, who told her that she thought I was "up to something again" and wouldn't be satisfied until I saw Hector behind bars. She was right about that, so I told Karen that I had an appointment with a police officer the following Monday and I would have them contact her. I didn't understand why Lydia was standing by Hector, especially when, according to what she had told Karen, they had a big fight a couple of days before.

He had told her to get out because he owned more of the house than she did. If the truth were told, Grandpa and Grandma owned more of the house than either of them, and the car too, since they had given him most of the money for both. Anyway, Hector had been verbally abusive to Lydia, which was no big surprise, and Marvin had confirmed to me previously that Hector was physically abusive to all of them. Again, I didn't understand why Lydia was standing by him when she knew that he was abusive to her children.

With Grandma still being so ill, Karen's conversation with Lydia had come around to the funeral. Lydia told Karen that Hector would be there and if I dared say anything to him she would make a scene. That was fine with me because the rest of the family wouldn't be standing behind him and at that point I would have welcomed the confrontation.

When I talked to Mom about it later however, she told me that if I couldn't hold my tongue I should stay home from the funeral. I was very upset to hear that, but since Grandma was still alive I would cross that bridge when I got to it. I couldn't believe that my mother actually thought I would miss the funeral. I agreed that it wasn't the time or place for a confrontation, but I wasn't going to back down if Hector or Lydia started anything.

I was feeling more confident in those days and I kept thinking that I felt more like myself, but I wasn't really sure who that was. Once my doctor had increased my dosage of Sinequan I was finally able to quit smoking, so I had gained some weight. It didn't really bother me except that my clothes were getting too tight and I didn't have the money to replace them with bigger ones. I started watching what I ate and did a short workout every day, not to lose weight as I had needed to gain a couple of pounds anyway, just to firm up the weight I already had and prevent gaining any more.

I started wearing makeup again as I had up until a year or so before. Back then I had never left the house without it. I never wore much, just mascara and lipstick and occasionally some light eye shadow and blush, but I felt more alive and awake with it on. My fingernails were growing again and that was a very good sign. Mom had once told me that she could tell how I was doing emotionally by the length of my nails. After that I started to notice that when my relationships went sour I would start biting my nails and once it was over they would grow long and lovely. I was caring more about myself than I had in a long time and not beating myself up about past mistakes.

I stopped by my cousin Marvin's one day to pick up the book I had loaned him and he asked if he could come over for a visit. I was happy to have him as we all adored him and the kids had a great day playing with him. He was teaching Tai Jitsu at the time and showing them some of the moves. Arthur wanted to take lessons and Marvin told him that he would need to take gymnastics first and then he would teach him.

Marvin was a wonderful young man and all day he kept saying how much he loved us too. He wanted to know when he and his girlfriend Krista could take the kids out for the day to the Science Center or someplace like it. I hadn't met Krista and didn't really know anything about her, but I trusted Marvin with them and they adored him. I told him anytime would be fine. He asked if I thought he would be a good father, as he really wanted to have children someday.

I thought his father's behavior worried him, like he would turn out the same way. I told him that I thought he would make a great daddy, and that the things his father had done were beyond the comprehension of decent people. In spite of his father he had grown up to be a very decent person. He seemed to have a lot of respect for Krista and their relationship, so I hoped he got what he wanted, even if it was with someone else later on.

I had always thought it strange that when Marvin was a child he had been sent off to a special school for emotionally disturbed children or those with behavioral problems. No doubt he qualified, but it seemed to me that his father was the one who needed help, as if a pedophile could be helped. I was amazed at how well Marvin had turned out and I believed that it was his faith in God that had helped him survive.

CHAPTER TWENTY-ONE

1992

The Family Tree

During one of my counseling sessions we were asked to make a diagram, like a family tree, and indicate with different colors, those who were victims and perpetrators or those whom we suspected were. I was shocked when I finished mine to see that there were many in my family. Some of those I suspected because sexual abuse is a learned behavior and I just had a gut feeling where the known perpetrators had learned it. Also there were parts of my life that I had blocked out, which Jasmine told me was common in abuse victims.

It happened because the memories were too traumatic for the mind to handle, so they were blocked out along with normal every day things that occurred during that period. I had chunks of time during my early childhood, before the age of twelve or so, that I had no memory of and although that concerned both Jasmine and I, she told me not to try to remember. My mind would let the memories come when and if it could handle whatever it was blocking out.

Of course I knew that my biological father George was a pedophile, since he had stuck his tongue down my throat when I was sixteen. That one act alone qualified him. I suspected he had learned that was okay from his father, my paternal grandfather. It followed that if he were a pedophile, George could have also been abused, along with his brother. I knew that George had abused my Aunt Jane, since that had been the reason my mother had finally left him.

I also suspected that perhaps one or both of my brothers had been abused in some way. I had no evidence of that, but Hector was also their uncle and they exhibited signs of a victim whenever the subject came up, showing the same rage that I had. Either that, or refusing to discuss the issue all together. People who had never suffered sexual abuse usually had no problem talking about it, even if it made them a little uncomfortable. I didn't seriously believe either one of them cared enough about me for the rage to be due to the fact that I had been molested. I had no proof that any of them were either victims or perpetrators, just a very strong feeling based on their behavior. An abuse victim can usually spot another one without too much trouble, seeing certain of their own behaviors reflected in the other.

I knew that Aunt Karen's husband Mike had been abused as a child, which may be what unknowingly attracted him to her. The old "birds of a feather", or like attracting like. Then of course, there were Aunt Karen, cousins Julie and Lynn, as well as myself that I knew were victims.

With Hector being a known perpetrator, his entire family became possible victims and also possible perpetrators as well. Once again, I couldn't fathom that my family thought that was something we should just sweep under the rug and it became obvious again that they had no idea the extent of damage this crime caused. I figured most other families probably didn't either, but extensive reading on the subject, along with personal experience, had convinced me that if there was one perpetrator in a family, there was sure to be more and victims as well. That was certainly true in my case.

Fortunately, I soon began my Cognitive Therapy group and right from the first session I could see how much it would help me. We were using a book called "The Feeling Good Handbook" by David D. Burns. One of the exercises that we had to do dealt with our emotions and thought processes. How to change how we felt by changing how we thought. It helped me to recognize when I was feeling a strong emotion and identify first what the emotion was, then the incident that had triggered that emotion. I began to recognize the irrational thoughts swimming around in my head that caused me to feel strong negative emotions. By recognizing the irrational thoughts and changing them to rational ones through self talk, I was able to reduce the emotion in a very short period of time.

At the same time I was still reading a lot of other self-help books and some of them dealt with the same thing. "The Dance of Anger" by Harriet Lerner dealt with anger and from it I learned that only I was responsible for feeling angry. Two reasons that people felt angry, it said, were because they felt they were being treated unfairly, or because there was some truth to what another person was saying. My anger was not hurting anyone other than myself, so it was not useful.

My biggest problem had always been feeling responsible for someone else's anger and doing my best not to upset people. It had always caused me severe stress, trying to please everyone all the time, especially men that I was in a relationship with. Of course I felt responsible for their anger; they told me that I was. I 'pushed their buttons' or 'pissed them off', so why wouldn't I feel responsible?

In therapy I was learning that if I was responsible for my own feelings, whatever they may be, then so was everyone else responsible for theirs. It would take time to actually understand and put it into practice, but I felt that if I could remember that lesson it would help me very much in my dealings with other people. I believed that you should treat others the way that you wished to be treated and would continue to do so. I had also let people, particularly men, walk all over me my whole life, because I was afraid they would get angry. That was about to change, and with it my life.

CHAPTER TWENTY-TWO

1992

A New Beginning, or Not

One thing that was recommended to me in therapy was gardening. I had always loved nature and had a garden whenever possible, so it was fortunate that at that time I was living in a house that had a backyard, with a small area beside the patio that I could turn into a garden. It was the perfect time of year for planting, so I set about digging, weeding and planting. I decided to grow vegetables rather than flowers and put those in the front yard instead. I was at a very low point in my life and my self-esteem was pretty much non-existent, so I took great joy in working in the garden, especially knowing that my little family would be able to enjoy the vegetables that I was growing.

One day as I was working in the garden, pulling out some weeds that were threatening to choke the tiny sprouts that were beginning to poke through the soil, I started thinking about my life.

It wasn't long before the tears came running down my cheeks, dripping onto the soil. I was feeling very alone and unloved and wondering once again why it was so hard to find someone who loved me just the way I was, unconditionally. What was wrong with me that I always had to change who I was to please people and earn their love? There had never been anyone who just loved me no matter what. Then it hit me. Yes there had been and I had turned my back on him and his love.

That's when I started thinking about my ex boyfriend Mason. No matter how down I felt he had always been able to make me smile and feel like things weren't so bad after all. Sometimes it had been really annoying, but for the most part had helped. I just needed a strong shoulder to cry on, until I couldn't cry anymore. I wanted so badly to pick up the phone and call him, but he was with someone else and I couldn't turn back time. I felt the need to just hear his voice telling me that everything would work out. I knew that I should be able to do that for myself, but I was feeling very weak and vulnerable and wanted his strength to help me.

****

Mason

I remembered back when I had been living with Jeff; one day while he was at work, there was a knock on the door. When I opened it, much to my surprise and chagrin, there stood Mason and some friend of his. That was not good, as I knew for a fact that Mason was serving time in prison and shouldn't be there. I hurried him into the house so I could get an explanation as to what he was doing there. He told me that he and his cellmate Garrett had been on an escorted pass to the city and had escaped from their guard. That was also not good news and I fully expected the police to be right behind them.

He wanted to borrow my car as they had arranged to get money from some friends of Garrett's, but had no way of getting there. Their plan was to get out of the country for awhile until things cooled down. I didn't want to help Mason, but he had a way of making me feel guilty and harassing me until I gave in to his demands. After a lot of talking on his part I finally agreed that they could borrow my car for a couple of hours, but that if they got caught with it, I would tell the police that they had taken it without my permission. He agreed, saying that he didn't want me to get into trouble with the law because of him. I couldn't help thinking that if that were true, why did he keep coming to me for help?

Just before he left, I told Mason that I had to have the car back before Jeff got home from work. He would be furious if he knew that Mason and his friend had been over at the house and that I had let them take the car. They left and said that they would be back in a couple of hours.

As it turned out, Mason came back to the house alone and had plans to meet with Garrett somewhere else later. He brought a bottle of rye with him and wanted me to have a drink, but I told him that I just wanted him to leave. It wasn't safe for either of us for him to be at my house.

The next thing I knew he was asking me to have sex with him before he left. I told him that I most certainly would not and he asked if I wanted him to beg. I said that he could beg all he wanted, but I would not change my answer. So he got down on his knees and actually started begging. I understood his persistence given our past history and the fact that he had been in jail for several years, but that didn't change the fact that I was in a relationship. Jeff had been faithful to me since he had screwed around at the beginning of our relationship. At least as far as I knew, so I wasn't going to disrespect him that way. I told Mason that he should just leave. He finally gave up and left to meet Garrett.

A couple of days later, I heard that they had been caught. They had only been on the run for three days at the time. They had spent those three days doing fraud to make money. They had roamed the local bars stoned on cocaine and flashing large rolls of cash. Gee, I couldn't see how they would get caught keeping such a low profile. Mason got another month added to his original sentence.

****

Afterwards I regretted that I had to refuse him, since we did have a great sex life when we had lived together, but there had been Jeff. Now Jeff was gone and I still had feelings for Mason. How I must have hurt him, marrying his

160

brother Max when he was begging me to marry him instead. How hard it must have been for him to know that every night I was lying beside his brother, making love and making plans for our children and our lives. The worst part had been that I married Max, not out of love, but simply so I would always be close to Mason. But, Mason was always in trouble with the law, in and out of jail and I just couldn't see a future for us.

Even when I ended my relationship with Max, I turned to Jeff and cut myself off from Mason, making myself unavailable to him. After all I had done that hurt him I knew that he still loved me. I thought about him a lot over the next few days and the more I did, the more I knew I had to find out either way if we still had a chance before I could move on with my life. I just had to figure out how to go about it.

AFTERWORD

I learned a lot about myself, and about this horrific crime while I was in therapy. I hope that every person who might even suspect abuse of this nature in their past will seek help, if you haven't already.

I have mentioned a book that helped me tremendously and I highly recommend reading it. It was written by E. Sue Blume and the title is "Secret Survivors – Uncovering Incest and It's Aftereffects in Women".

While this is not an issue specific to women, as a woman I felt as though it were written just for me. I finally began to understand some of my attitudes and behaviours.

The aftereffects of incest are very similar to those of adults who grow up with alcoholic parents. Since alcohol was not a part of my childhood and I grew up in a very close, loving family, I knew that it had to be something else that had scarred me. For many years I had no idea I was being affected by what my uncle had done to me. It just wasn't talked about back then. Thankfully, incest is no longer the secret it used to be and victims are now able to get help as adults, even if they didn't have resources to turn to as children.

I can only speak from my own personal experience, so I would like to point out the aftereffects that I found in myself so that you also can understand them better:

First of all, there is a misconception as to the meaning of "incest". The majority believes that it is only sexual abuse by a parent, or at least a person that we are closely related to, but that is incorrect. Incest is sexual activity between an adult that a child depends on or trusts, like a caretaker. It definitely includes relatives, but also includes those like sports coaches, teachers, doctors and ministers -

anyone that the child has an emotional bond with. It is for this reason that incest is the most devastating form of child abuse. It doesn't just violate a child's body, it destroys boundaries and trust. These are the people that a child looks to for protection and safety. So when we can't trust our caretakers, who can we trust?

In the case of my uncle, he wasn't someone that I particularly liked as I had always found him creepy. However, he was a member of my family and therefore entrusted with my care at times. As for my father, even though I didn't grow up with him, I still always knew that he was my biological father and should have been able to trust him. He had abandoned me as a child, but when I found him as a teenager, I naturally assumed that I was safe with him.

I still don't know if there was ever any sexual abuse on his part before he left, but the fact that he stuck his tongue down my throat later was enough to obliterate my trust of him. Aside from the fact that he was my father, I was only sixteen years old. Although I was no longer a virgin, my sexual activity was not with adult males, but with boys my own age, as it should be. I will never forgive my father for that, nor will I forgive my uncle.

I have no intention of trying to unblock any memories of my childhood if indeed there are any. I am able to lead a reasonably normal life and it would serve no purpose. My family has already proven that they would not be supportive of my efforts to get justice. The law has already failed me in the past and likely could do no better now. I have chosen to move on and let the memories stay where they are.

Incest also does not necessarily involve touching, as in my mother's case. She told me that "he showed me things that little girls shouldn't be shown" and it has the same effect as touching. Although the man that abused her was not related, he was a deacon in our church and someone that she should have been able to trust. Whenever a child is exposed to anything with sexual overtones, it is a violation of their innocence and creates the same aftereffects later in life.

Violence and threats are also not necessary for it to be considered abuse. As a child, one believes that the adult knows better and that they have no choice but to allow the abuse. Whether or not that is true is irrelevant, as long as the child believes it to be true. Having to keep this horrible secret creates many problems for a child as they become ashamed that they participated in the sexual activity. I know that for many years I felt that I had somehow encouraged my uncle's behavior, or that his wife had by being unable to satisfy him sexually. Others blame their mothers and I am so sick of hearing that.

An adult male is responsible for his own behavior, and nobody else. In some cases the child does feel more betrayal from the mother, feeling that her mother should have noticed something was wrong and protected her. Many who go to therapy for incest end up doing years of therapy on clearing up issues with the mother even if it was the father that did the real damage. That's why in later years they end up not trusting women and competing with them over men. I had never felt betrayed by my mother, just disappointed that she hadn't been strong enough to deal with her own abuse. Other women that I know however, were still very angry at their mother for not helping them.

As in my family, incest rarely stops at one act, or one victim. The perpetrator does not truly believe that what he is doing is wrong, only that society says it is. He will keep his secret and continue until he is forced to stop. The only way to force him to stop is to remove him from society, which sadly I was unable to do. Also, there is usually more than one perpetrator in a family. It is a learned behavior and often the child grows up to repeat the abuse with other children. Of course not all victims become abusers. The effect that this crime had on my life is something that I could never conceive doing to another person. Unfortunately, some victims go on to become perpetrators themselves.

Even when a victim doesn't become a perpetrator, their own children and the children that follow are at risk of becoming victims themselves. How can one teach another that they are valued if they are not themselves valued? How can one teach their child that they have a right to say no, when they themselves don't know how? You cannot teach what you don't know and instilling self-esteem in a child is impossible when you have lost yours. Sadly, this did pass on to future generations in my family, as it does in many others.

Another important after effect, is that in many cases the child's emotional development is arrested at the time of the abuse. It took me many years to develop beyond the age of 14 emotionally and even at age 50 I sometimes struggle with it. I find it very difficult sometimes to react appropriately to emotional situations, particularly involving sex and romantic love. I also struggle with having my own needs fulfilled. I was taught as a child that my needs didn't matter, only the needs of my abuser. I was there for his pleasure and nothing else.

I was not important and had no value as an individual, except to satisfy a man's sexual needs. I learned that I had no power and that my needs not only didn't matter, they weren't even heard. That has been devastasting to my life as I struggled through several relationships, living as someone else's doormat. I became invisible and for many years as a teenager wore mainly black clothing. It drove my mother crazy that I didn't like the colored clothes that she bought me. Black made me feel safe, like I was less likely to attract attention. I wore a lot of turtlenecks, long sleeved shirts and long pants. I preferred not to show my body in case it attracted the attention of some male that wanted to have sex.

As I got older I discovered that by having sex with men they would love me. At least that was what I believed. It was very difficult for me to discern between love and sex.

The line was blurry. To me sex was love and a way to get what I wanted. Most of the time I just wanted the man to leave me alone, but since my needs didn't matter, I wasn't able to refuse sex on his terms. I learned that in order to be loved I had to produce and without sexual favors I had nothing to offer a man. I remember very few times in my life that I actually enjoyed sex, just for the sake of enjoying it. There always seemed to be pressure to perform at a man's will, whether I wanted to or not, which enforced the belief that I was invisible. I was there to take care of the man and nothing more, even though I had children to take care of.

As with children of alcoholic parents, victims of incest suffer with control and boundary issues, depression, anxiety, co-dependence, assertiveness and a sense of being responsible for everything that happens around them. These are all problems that I struggled with throughout my life, and sometimes still do. Even though I have grown into an adult, the effects have not all been healed by time. They are always close to the surface. Intellectually I know right from wrong, but emotionally there is much confusion on a constant basis. It feels as though the child I was ceased to exist and was replaced with a different person. I have spent many hours mourning that child and wishing that she had been allowed to live. It truly is death for the child victim, of her body and her soul.

I have found some happiness in my life and at least on the surface, am slow to anger. Underneath the surface however, is a burning rage that never goes away. At times it scares me to think of what I could be capable of were I to turn it loose. I hide my anger partly due to fear of confrontation, but on the occasions that I have shown it, the rage bursts forth and I don't recognize the person that I become. Guilt always follows, so I go back to containing the anger, lest it turn to rage.

And Sew it Begins is only part one or book one of my story. It will be continued through the series, *Shadows of the*

Mind. As you continue with future books, you will get further insight into the devastating effects of incest which have led to promiscuity, drug and alcohol addiction. You will notice that each of these 'symptoms' began around age 14, shortly after the last incidence of abuse. Those in turn led to a period of domestic violence as well as a constant struggle with depression. By reading each book, you will follow in my footsteps and begin to notice for yourself how the horrible patterns of incest keep weaving their way back into my life. It is a constant and vigilant struggle. I felt that rather then spell everything out for the people I am trying to reach, it would be better understood if they were with me every step of the way.

Writing the series, *Shadows of the Mind*, is a very difficult experience. It brings childhood emotions back to the surface for me. At times I have had to relive the experiences I wish to forget. Then there have been times where I needed to leave the material behind for some time and return to it when I was once again grounded in my present life – that of the adult. I remind myself often that I am an adult now and the men that hurt and sexually abused me can no longer hurt me. I am in charge now. That is the power I have gained and the truth I have come to understand, that I can and have empowered myself over my past.

Even in the writing of this series I struggled with the decision of whether to use my real name or a pen name. I finally decided that by using a pen name I would be letting him win by keeping me invisible. I am no longer afraid and decided to use my real name. I am not invisible and have a right to be heard. I did however, change the names of everyone else in order to protect the innocent. The guilty I don't really care about.

Do all victims suffer these after effects? No, it is different for everyone. Some victims actually go on to lead productive lives, which I feel I have in many ways. There is however a common thread – all incest victims more or less struggle with love relationships. I still do not know if I will find a truly loving, lasting relationship with the opposite sex, nor am I sure I really want to at this point. Only time can tell and it may be a few years before I know the answer to that question.

Watch for

Book Two

in the

SHADOWS OF THE MIND

series.

Between the Crack

Journey of an Addict

COMING SOON